Deb Bickford

The First-Year Experience
Monograph Series No. 33

Proving and Improving

Strategies for Assessing the First College Year

Randy L. Swing

Editor

NATIONAL RESOURCE CENTER FOR THE FIRST-YEAR EXPERIENCE® & STUDENTS IN TRANSITION
UNIVERSITY OF SOUTH CAROLINA, 2001

Cite as:

Swing, R. L. (Ed.). (2001). *Proving and improving: Strategies for assessing the first college year* (Monograph No. 33). Columbia, SC: University of South Carolina, National Resource Center for The First-Year Experience and Students in Transition.

Sample chapter citation:

Upcraft, M. L., & Schuh, J. H. (2001). Assessing the first-year student experience: A framework. In R. L. Swing (Ed.), *Proving and improving: Strategies for assessing the first college year* (Monograph No. 33) (pp. 7-9). Columbia, SC: University of South Carolina, National Resource Center for The First-Year Experience and Students in Transition.

The Freshman Year Experience® and The First-Year Experience® are service marks of the University of South Carolina. A license may be granted upon written request to use the terms The Freshman Year Experience and The First-Year Experience. This license is not transferrable without written approval of the University of South Carolina.

Additional copies of this monograph may be from the National Resource Center for The First-Year Experience and Students in Transition, University of South Carolina, 1728 College Street, Columbia, SC 29208. Telephone (803) 777-6029. Telefax (803) 777-4699.

Special gratitude is expressed to Tracy L. Skipper, Editorial Projects Coordinator, for the editing, design, and layout of this book; to Jean M. Henscheid, Associate Director, for editing; and to Scott Slawinski, Editorial Assistant, for copy editing.

Proving and improving : strategies for assessing the first college year / Randy L. Swing, editor.
    p. cm. -- (The first-year experience monograph series ; no. 33)
   Includes bibliographic references.
   ISBN 1-889271-37-3 (alk. paper)
   1. College student development programs--Evaluation. 2. College freshmen. 3. Educational tests and measurements. I. Swing, Randy L., 1954- II. Series.

LB2324.4 .P78 2001
378.1'98--dc21   2001044846

Table of Contents

Part 3
Program & Institutional Examples

Part 4
Conclusions & Recommendations

Preface

John N. Gardner

The Policy Center on the First Year of College was established on October 18, 1999, to work with colleges and universities around the nation to develop and share a range of first-year assessment procedures and tools. Our work is currently funded through the generous support of The Atlantic Philanthropies and The Pew Charitable Trusts. These procedures and tools will be used to measure the effectiveness of existing institutional programs, policies, and structures that affect first-year students. The data collected using these tools will help build a body of information on best practices in the first college year, and the findings will be disseminated to other campuses that desire to increase student success as measured by academic performance and retention. The founding of this Center is an outgrowth of my work at the University of South Carolina (USC) from 1970 to 1999 and the work of the Policy Center's co-directors, Betsy Barefoot (The National Resource Center, from 1988 to 1999) and Randy L. Swing (Appalachian State University, from 1980 to 1999).

Based on our work with other colleges and universities, the Policy Center staff has concluded that we are sadly in need of better assessment data pertaining to the first college year. We are particularly encouraging the idea of treating the first college year as a unit of assessment, per se. We seek to engage our colleagues in stepping back and looking at the forest, the entire first year, as opposed to just individual trees, or components, within the forest. We believe that we need far more information about what works and what does not work in terms of increasing student learning, success, satisfaction, and retention as a result of the first-year experience. The first college year is the foundation of the entire undergraduate experience, and we still have much to learn about it. In order to expand our collective knowledge of what does and does not work to enhance student learning during this critical period, the Policy Center, with technical support from the University of South Carolina and the staff of the National Resource Center for The First-Year Experience and Students in Transition, sponsored a series of invited postings from nationally known educators, researchers, and assessment experts. The inspiration for the First-Year Assessment (FYA) Listserv came from my colleague Randy Swing, who served as primary facilitator of the list. But as often happens when using technology, what actually developed was not an open forum for online conversations about the topic.

Instead, the FYA-List morphed into an online magazine containing essays and reports from some of the top thinkers in the emerging field of first-year assessment.

The Policy Center is also very interested in creating partnerships among faculty, academic administrators, student affairs professionals, institutional research directors/staff members, and colleagues involved in all aspects of institutional self-study. Unfortunately, it has been our observation, in our work with thousands of colleagues around the country to improve the learning of first-year college students, that institutional research experts have been largely absent from the conversation on assessing the first college year. We hope that the Policy Center and the listserv we initiated will be able to bring significant numbers of our institutional research colleagues into this important national conservation about improving the success of first-year college students. All of us in assessment know that we need better tools and resources to assess the impact of the first college year. Developing those tools and resources is the primary mission of the Policy Center.

To that end, the early work of the Policy Center focused on the development and/or use of a number of tools for assessment. The first one was an instrument entitled Your First College Year, a follow-up to the Higher Education Research Institute's Freshman Survey. The second was a national survey developed by my colleague, Betsy Barefoot, to collect and report information about current practices in the first year (see the Policy Center's web site for a report on the survey's findings). The third tool we used was the Performance Analyzer, a technological tool that uses focus groups to collect data on the first-year experience. We have also developed, in cooperation with Educational Benchmarking, Inc., a national benchmarking instrument on first-year seminars, "First-Year Facilitation." Last, with the guidance of five institutional consortia involving 65 institutions in three states, the Policy Center revised and disseminated a template for evaluating the first college year called *Guidelines for Evaluating the First-Year Experience*, recently published by the National Resource Center for The First-Year Experience and Students in Transition. Several of these projects were addressed in postings to the listserv and will be revisited in this volume.

During my quarter century directorship for the first-year seminar course at the University of South Carolina, one of the lessons I learned was that assessment was the key to the success and institutionalization of this initiative. In 1972, we developed a freshman seminar known as University 101, which became the benchmark for the freshman seminar concept in American higher education. We succeeded at this, not because we had extraordinary stability in terms of one faculty director for a quarter of a century, but because we successfully developed an assessment process for measuring the institutional effectiveness of this course. So, I am a true believer in the power of assessment.

As we launched the FYA listserv, we hoped to engage participants in a dialogue about a number of what we thought were very compelling questions. I believe these are still important questions, and this monograph will provide some context for them. These questions are:

1. What do you know about the first-year experience on your campus and in general?
2. How do you know what you know? What processes did you use to come to these conclusions?
3. What are you doing with this information?

4. How are you using it to influence institutional decision making and resource allocation?
5. What can you share with others about how you got started in your assessment process of the first college year, what obstacles you encountered, and how you overcame them?
6. What would you like to know from others about improving assessment of the first college year?

In addition to these questions, we simply need to inquire further into the period when we take in and lose the most students. We also need to acquire more information on the effectiveness of the first-year experience, particularly as it relates to what I have called "the senior-year experience." For example, how can we intellectually and specifically connect what we do at the beginning of the college experience to what we want the student outcomes to be at the conclusion of that experience? Answers to these questions are urgently needed throughout higher education because they can help to shape institutional thinking and decisions about resource allocation and can have a real impact on the educational experiences of our students.

Best wishes to you on your assessment work from those of us here at the Policy Center on the First Year of College in Brevard, North Carolina and the National Resource Center on The First-Year Experiences and Students in Transition at the University of South Carolina. We hope the original, albeit slightly revised, listserv postings included here will be the beginning of a helpful, lively, and thoughtful national discussion on issues that pertain to improving assessment of the first college year.

John N. Gardner, Executive Director
Policy Center on the First Year of College
Brevard College

Senior Fellow
National Resource Center for The First-Year Experience and Students in Transition
University of South Carolina
July 2001

Introduction

Randy L. Swing

First-year programs that survive and thrive likely share a common link—a strong outcome assessment agenda that is closely connected to program goals. Simply put, assessment findings provide protection and leverage in hard times and guidance for improvement anytime. John Gardner, Betsy Barefoot, and others have observed that first-year seminars and other programs serving large numbers of first-year students (e.g., advising, orientation, residence life, learning communities) are asked to "prove their value" more frequently than high status, discipline-based programs. "Proving and improving" is not a luxury for first-year programs but a core element of success, a natural extension of professional curiosity, and an essential expression of respect for our students.[1] It is paramount that assessment undergirds the structure of first-year programs as an integral component rather than simply be "bolted on" as an after thought.

Actual use of assessment practice varies widely across institutions and first-year programs. Results from a study of current educational practices conducted by the Policy Center on the First Year of College found that 92% of orientation programs, 87% of residence life units, 64% of Greek life programs, and 63% of academic advising programs are regularly evaluated. These results show that evaluation of first-year services is common but certainly not ubiquitous. Additional analyses reveal the limited use of assessment in the first college year. For example, among residence life programs, the vast majority (86%) focus assessment efforts on student satisfaction. A much smaller percent assess the impact of residence life on other important educational outcomes such as retention (37%), academic performance (31%), student involvement (18%), or social development (7%). Although measuring multiple outcomes associated with a phenomenon represents best practice in assessment, only 33% of residence life units regularly study three or more outcomes (24% study two, 33% study only one, and 10% study none). In similar fashion, only 36% of Greek life programs study two or more outcomes.

In practice, assessment of first-year programs is frequently limited to two forms: surveys of student satisfaction and correlation analyses of participation and one-year

ix

enrollment attrition. Such studies can be quite important but, unfortunately, are too often poorly designed and inadequately reported so that little is changed as a result of the effort. If the preeminent objective of assessment is informing change or confirming established practice, then assessment results must be both useful and used.

Because of the crucial role assessment plays in developing, improving, and sustaining first-year programs, the Policy Center on the First Year of College was established to develop and disseminate assessment strategies to improve the first-year experience of college students. Generous grants from the Atlantic Philanthropic Corporation and The Pew Charitable Trusts enable Policy Center staff to develop new assessment instruments, conduct national conferences, and create consortia to support innovative assessment techniques focused on first-year students. One of those initiatives, a listserv focusing on first-year assessment issues, begun by John Gardner, Betsy Barefoot, and myself in partnership with The National Resource Center on The First-Year Experience and Students in Transition, attracted some 300 subscribers during the first three days of existence. After only one month, participants on the First-Year Assessment List (FYA-List) numbered 600 and a few months later topped 800 subscribers. The FYA-List evolved into a kind of online magazine, delivering an array of scholarly and thoughtful essays to list members via e-mail and archives on the World Wide Web. Those postings, contributed by invited assessment scholars and practitioners, formed the foundation for this collection of scholarly essays.

The essays included in this collection were written for an online audience and were designed to stimulate discussion on the topic of first-year assessment practice. Thus, they are shorter and more informal in their tone than might be expected from assessment scholarship. In most cases, only minor changes have been made in the original versions of these essays. The most frequent changes include the addition of citations, the removal of language more appropriate to the online environment, and the incorporation of documents hyper-linked to the original essay. What has not been changed is the generosity and enthusiasm with which the essays were originally posted to the FYA-List.

Several themes emerge from the essays contributed to the FYA-List and selected for this monograph.

1. The reason for conducting assessment is to promote student learning and success—not simply to collect data (Suskie). Assessment and program improvement are inseparably linked in the best assessment efforts.

2. A body of best practices in assessment of first-year programs—a solid foundation upon which to base our efforts—exists (Barefoot, Cuseo, Gardner, Porter). Because such a foundation has been established, "ignorance is no longer an excuse" (Kuh). We have an array of tools and techniques on which to base assessment efforts.

3. Best practice in first-year assessment includes, indeed necessitates, collaboration. The most useful assessment efforts combine a host of skills and strategies. Thus, the call for professional partnerships among and between faculty, student affairs professionals, institutional researchers, and assessment officers is a basic theme in these essays (Bers, Baughman & Swing, Levine, Schilling, Terenzini). Professors, academic administrators, student development professionals, and institutional researchers working in collaboration combine skills in statistics, research design, student development and pedagogical theories, and more. Assessment is best when collaboration occurs across traditional campus unit and organizational lines.

4. A culture of assessment can be developed where decision makers—academic leaders, student affairs officers, and teaching faculty—use evidence to inform policy and practice. Assessment can build on the natural curiosity that draws us to academic lives. We must be willing to ask and answer questions about our own work (Ewell, Upcraft & Schuh). Basic to assessment is having clear program goals and tightly linking assessment to those goals (Levine).

5. Assessment is best when it is grounded in theory (Palomba, Schroeder) and grows from focused questions. There are too many important questions to waste time simply "fishing around" in hopes of hooking a big one! Theory can guide the selection of assessment questions so that we focus on what is really important for accomplishing our program goals. Theories and practices from outside the academy, such as benchmarking (Detrick & Pica) and strategic planning strategies (Moore), commonly used in business settings, can be usefully adapted to higher education institutions.

6. Assessment must include the student voice and adapt to the realities of student experiences (Bers, Schilling, Schroeder, Upcraft & Schuh). Best practice in assessment maintains the goodwill of students and honors their input in the process and in the reporting of outcomes (Palomba).

7. Room exists for both high-tech and low-tech assessment methods. Recent developments in computer-enhanced assessment methods, including software, hardware, and national databases, offer new opportunities to increase the accuracy of data collection, reduce intrusion into the lives of students, and disseminate findings to key decisions makers in highly useful formats (Baughman & Swing, Kuh, Porter, Swing).

8. The first college year is a dynamic environment that is best evaluated with multiple measures rather than single snapshots (Levine, Porter, Suskie).

These themes highlight general agreement about best practice in first-year assessment, but this collection contains some differences of opinion as well. Readers will find both arguments for using external evaluators as the best method for providing unbiased and credible evidence (Upcraft & Schuh, Detrick & Pica) and arguments for using insiders who know the programs, understand the students, and have a vested interest in program development (Cuseo). These divergent views note the strengths of each strategy but do not create a false dichotomy. Rather, such differences simply provide further support for using multiple assessment methods.

This monograph acknowledges that assessing first-year programs for the purpose of improvement is a relatively young scholarly activity that builds on two of the great traditions of first-year programs. The first is the spirit of sharing that has permeated the first-year culture. The authors of these essays willingly share insights and lessons learned. These are scholarly trailblazers who share their stories as markers for other scholars and practitioners traveling the assessment path. The second tradition is the balance of challenge and support, a common theme across first-year programs. Readers will find that there are no silver bullets and few short cuts in creating high quality assessment results, but they will also find inspiration and practical advice for making assessment work.

The essays are organized into four sections.[2] The first section contains essays of general philosophical and practical considerations. Each article focuses on the importance of a particular aspect of assessment. The second section provides advice about implementing assessment. These articles are very practical strategies for conducting assessment and reporting results. The third section highlights assessment of three particular curricular structures (first-year seminars, learning communities, and general education programs.) The fourth section provides suggestions and predictions for the future.

Combined, these sections provide a brief exploration of a wide range of topics associated with first-year assessment. Readers will find a mix of rationales for how and why to do assessment, methods and tools for assessment, and specific program and institutional examples. In the spirit of the listserv from which these essays are drawn, this collection is not meant to be an ending point but a starting point. As Gardner suggests in his preface to this volume, we hope to involve educators in an ongoing conversation about assessment rather than speaking the final words on the topic. Most importantly, these essays confirm the central importance of assessment in supporting success in the first year of college. Our first-year students deserve no less than our best efforts at promoting student satisfaction and learning.

Notes

[1] I would like to acknowledge Jean MacGregor's contribution in identifying proving and improving as two closely related assessment agendas in her 1995 essay "Going Public: How Collaborative Learning and Learning Communities Invite New Assessment Approaches."

[2] The organizational structure for this monograph was developed by Tracy L. Skipper, Editorial Projects Coordinator at the National Resource Center for The First-Year Experience and Students in Transition. Her guidance and creative arrangement are core components of this monograph.

Part 1

Overview & Rationale

Observations on Assessing The First-Year Experience

Peter Ewell

As John Gardner quite rightly points out in his preface to this collection, those involved in The First-Year Experience movement over the past two decades have dedicated their efforts to programs that work, but they have been less systematic about developing an information infrastructure to determine whether or exactly how those programs work. Here, I will offer a few observations designed to help educators working with first-year programs address this need.

First, we must recognize just how important information about implementation and results will be in the next few years. As external accountability demands grow from state legislatures and from accrediting bodies, explicit questions are being asked about program effectiveness. Any data are helpful here, but those dealing with the effectiveness of a large, multifaceted program such as The First-Year Experience—a program that affects large numbers of students—will be especially welcome. At the same time, budgets will be tight, and every program will be under pressure to demonstrate its effectiveness to institutional decision makers. Finally, assessment in the first year can help set the stage for assessment throughout the institution—modeling the concept of a "culture of evidence" and building databases that can be gradually extended for more general institutional use.

Second, it is useful to frame assessment of the first year in terms of two quite different overriding questions: What happened? and What mattered? The first of these has to do with implementation and raises the often-overlooked issue of the degree to which prototypes and designs are actually acted out in the field. This becomes especially important as a program is scaled up to include multiple sections and large numbers of students. I am always struck by the appropriateness of Joan Stark's aphorism about the "three curricula" present at any college—the one that's in the catalog, the one the faculty actually teaches, and the one the students actually experience (Stark & Lowther, 1986). The First-Year Experience is like that as well, and it is wise to invest considerable assessment resources during the initial phases of program implementation to find out about the curricula that are "not in the catalog." Generally this involves fairly "soft" data, including quick in-class questionnaires like those suggested by Angelo and Cross (1993), focus group interviews, and classroom observation. The second assessment question—"What mattered?"—addresses the actual learning that took place. Here we get into more classic methods of learning assessment such as performance in later coursework, direct assessments of cognitive gain in such areas as communications and math, as well as various areas of affective development that can be tapped by surveys and interview methods (Palomba & Banta, 1999).

Third, the answer to the question of "What mattered?" depends a lot on what was originally intended. The goals of a first-year experience program are nothing if not complicated. When thinking about whether or not goals have been attained, for instance, I like quickly to make a list of the often quite different things that any first-year experience is trying to accomplish. A beginning list of intended outcomes might include:

1. *Foundational skills development.* These are cognitive abilities needed for later academic success such as writing, quantitative reasoning, and critical thinking that can be directly assessed at the end of a given course via examinations, exercises, or portfolio exhibits.
2. *Attributes associated with "negotiating college."* These center on basic knowledge of a particular college environment such as advisement, use of the library and other information resources, or counseling resources typically associated with student orientation. They are best assessed in terms of specific inventories of such knowledge administered early in the first year but can also be indirectly assessed through overall retention and success rates.
3. *Qualities associated with understanding the nature of academic life.* These center on academic good practices such as study habits and how to organize an academic project, as well as broader questions related to understanding the nature of scholarly work itself. Reflective essays, journal entries, and interviews are often of value here.
4. *Non-cognitive abilities.* Many first-year programs attempt to foster self-confidence, respect for diversity, and teamwork—qualities that will be useful not only in later academic work but also in the workplace and social settings. In-class exercises, inventories, questionnaires, and focus groups are often prominent assessment methods of these abilities.

Fourth, it is important to begin thinking of research on the first-year experience as an ongoing project, not a series of one-shot studies. This is where, as Gardner suggests elsewhere in this collection, the involvement of institutional researchers can be critical. In most cases, these professionals will have the capacity to construct integrated cohort data files. Such data files assemble important information about a given body of entering students, including their demographics, educational backgrounds, goals and expectations (drawn from surveys), and data on important experiences in the first year, like courses taken and results of any additional surveys that might be administered. Assembled in a single data file, this information can provide the means to conduct powerful studies of differential impact and can position the college for continuing longitudinal tracking into the later years of college.

Finally, the exercise of assessment must begin with a careful inventory of the information you may already have about first-year students. I am continually amazed when I visit campuses for the first time by how much data they have about the student experience that they are not using for assessment purposes—or may not even know about. Because particular offices responsible for particular functions often gather data from students on their own without letting anybody else know, these data are used only for their original, limited purposes. What is needed, instead, is a coordinated approach that begins with a formal inventory of who is collecting what, on whom, and at what time. We call this a "data audit" and highly recommend it as a first step for any campus that is beginning an assessment effort. And it is especially salient for evaluating the first-year experience because so much depends on establishing a good set of data on baseline conditions from which to conduct an ongoing longitudinal study on impact.

Most sound assessment efforts start small but are continually guided in their development by a few core questions. Thinking concretely about two core questions— "What happened?" and "What mattered?"—and how your particular campus might address them is a good place to begin.

References

Angelo, T. A., & Cross, K. P. (1993). *Classroom assessment techniques* (2nd ed.). San Francisco: Jossey-Bass.

Palomba, C. A., & Banta, T. W. (1999). *Assessment essentials*. San Francisco: Jossey-Bass.

Stark, J. S., & Lowther, M. (1986). *Designing the learning plan: A review of research and theory related to college curricula*. Ann Arbor, MI: NCRPTL, University of Michigan.

Assessing the First-Year Student Experience: A Framework

**M. Lee Upcraft &
John H. Schuh**

While we most certainly identify as researchers and scholars of the student experience, we are, at heart, practitioners. From an assessment standpoint, then, we think Peter Ewell is right on when he asks, "What happened?" and "What mattered?" Put in practitioner's terms, we translate this to mean: "How do I know if what I did to enhance first-year student success worked?" In our book *Assessment in Student Affairs: A Guide for Practitioners* (1996), we suggest a comprehensive model for assessing student services and programs. We believe that model can be adapted to an eight-part framework for assessing a variety of first-year programs.

1. Who Participates in Programs and Services?

The first component of this framework is keeping track of who participates in first-year student programs. How many students took advantage of each program and service targeted to first-year students, and how are they described by gender, race, ethnicity, age, residence, major, and other characteristics? This component is very important, because if first-year students do not participate, then our intended purposes cannot be achieved. But numbers do not tell the full story, because we must know if participants are representative of all first-year students, and if not, which ones are underrepresented.

2. What Do Students Need?

The second component is assessing student needs. Too often, we develop programs and services for first-year students that we believe meet their needs, but we seldom assess those needs in any systematic way. What kinds of services and programs do first-year students really need, based on student and staff perceptions, institutional expectations, and research on student needs? Put another way, how do we know if what we offer "fits" our first-year students? Assessing first-year student needs can provide answers to these questions and ensure that programs meet those needs.

3. Are Students Satisfied?

A third component is assessing first-year student satisfaction, which is the cornerstone of maintaining and improving the quality of services and programs targeted to first-year students. Of those first-year students who participate, what is their level of satisfaction? What strengths and suggestions for improvement do they identify? If students are dissatisfied, they will not reuse what we offer, and they will not recommend our services and programs to other students.

4. What Is the Campus Environment Like for First-Year Students?

A fourth component is assessing campus environments. While assessing individual use, needs, and satisfaction is important, understanding first-year students' collective perceptions of the campus environments within which they conduct their day-to-day lives enhances the meaning of these other findings. For example, what is the campus climate for first-year women? What is the academic environment, both inside and outside the classroom? What is the overall quality of life for first-year students in residence halls? Is the campus safe? Such assessments can provide valuable information for developing and revising first-year student programs and services.

5. What Outcomes Are Present?

A fifth component is assessing outcomes. Of those students who participate in services and programs targeted to first-year students, is there any effect on their learning, development, academic success, transition to college, retention, or other desired outcomes, particularly when compared with non-participants? Can these interventions be isolated from other variables that may influence outcomes, such as (a) students' characteristics and backgrounds before enrollment and (b) other first-year experiences that may affect these outcomes? These kinds of studies are difficult to design, implement, and interpret, but in some ways they attempt to answer the most basic question of all: Is what we are doing for and with first-year students having any effects, and if so, were they the intended ones?

6. How Does Our Institution Compare to Similar Institutions?

A sixth component is comparable institution assessment. How does the variety, quality, and impact of services and programs targeted to first-year students compare with "best in class" interventions at comparable institutions? And if our efforts do not measure up to other institutions, how might we improve those efforts based on what they are doing? The key to this component, however, is to select institutions that are (a) truly comparable and (b) have assessment-based evidence which confirms the efficacy of their programs and services.

7. How Do Our Programs and Services Compare to "Industry" Standards?

A seventh component is using nationally accepted standards to assess our efforts. How do the services and programs targeted to first-year students compare to accepted national standards, such as those developed by the Council for the Advancement of Standards for Student Services/Development Programs (CAS)?

In conjunction with the National Orientation Directors Association (NODA), CAS has developed a self-assessment protocol based on minimum standards for student orientation that includes mission, program, leadership, organization and management, human resources, financial resources, facilities/technology/equipment, legal responsibilities, equal opportunity/access/affirmative action, campus and community relations, diversity, ethics, and assessment/evaluation.

8. Do the Benefits to Students Outweigh the Costs Associated with Providing Programs and Services?

A final component is assessing cost effectiveness. Are the benefits students and the institution derive from the programs and services targeted to first-year students worth the cost and how do we know? Such systematic "cost/benefit" studies are seldom done, partly because "costs" are sometimes difficult to determine, and "benefits" are hard to measure in dollars. Nevertheless, the resource issue is a primary one and should be addressed in any comprehensive assessment of the first-year student experience.

The questions explored in this discussion provide a framework for assessing the first-year experience. The questions provide a comprehensive approach to assessment that may be more complex than is possible, given the normal demands on the time and resources of most units in student affairs. As a consequence, we recommend that assessments be conducted on a periodic basis, so that over a period of years a comprehensive array of assessments has been completed. For example, in Year 1, keeping track of participation rates and identifying student needs would make sense. That can be followed in Year 2 with assessments of student satisfaction and the impact of various programs and services. Environmental assessments might be scheduled every four or five years. Assessments examining cost effectiveness and comparing programs with similar institutions or industry standards similarly can be conducted every few years. Exactly how and when to conduct assessment will be influenced by the exigencies of individual campuses and specific programs. What is most important, in our view, is that assessments be integrated into the annual work routine, so that answers to Peter Ewell's questions of "What happened?" and "What mattered?" are provided regularly.

Reference

Upcraft, M. L., & Schuh, J. H. (1996). *Assessment in student affairs: A guide for practitioners.* San Francisco: Jossey-Bass.

Collaboration: The Key to Visible and Credible Assessment Efforts

Patrick T. Terenzini

Each contribution in this collection has stimulated my thinking about how assessment might be improved. In particular, the contributions have pushed me to think harder about why current assessment efforts do not seem to be contributing as much as I think they can/should to inform decision-making or to enhance program effectiveness and student learning (in a lot of areas).

Elsewhere in this collection, Peter Ewell prompts a particular line of thought with his sound advice to begin any assessment program with a careful inventory of the information that may already be available but unused. Lee Upcraft and John Schuh lay out a very helpful, eight-part framework for developing an effective assessment program. One explanation for assessment's limited impact is probably not any shortage of appropriate models, methods, and measures. Later in this collection, George Kuh identifies several useful measures (to which one might add those available through ACT, ETS, and UCLA's Higher Education Research Institute). Trudy Banta has published a couple of fine books on assessment methods and programs that work. Thinking about Ewell's recommendation, I conclude that the problem lies, at least in part, in our neglect of what is already available to us, including not only the resources just mentioned and the studies and information that may already be available on our campuses, but also many others as well. Some of those resources are right under our noses.

Many assessment efforts are, I think, less than fully successful in facilitating organizational and programmatic effectiveness because their fruits suffer from either or both of two conditions: (1) people do not know about them (hence, the need to follow Ewell's advice), or (2) they are not credible (having faulty conceptual, methodological, or political foundations). Assessment studies that are credibly done but unknown to people in positions to act on the findings are useless and a waste of scarce resources. Studies that are known but not methodologically credible are embarrassing liabilities to future efforts to continue or initiate other assessment activities. Studies that are neither credible nor known should be buried after dark, and those that are both credible and known should get wide campus attention.

Fortunately, I think a vaccine for both obscurity and non-credibility is readily available: collaboration. Space precludes detailed discussion of the form(s) such collaboration might take (and I'm not very clear on what I think about that anyway). My instincts tell me that local customs, conditions, and personalities should guide reforms. My point is really more a plea to involve faculty members, academic and student affairs administrators, and institutional researchers systematically in joint, cooperative efforts to determine campus assessment needs, to develop appropriate research designs and data collection plans, and to share in the discussion and "meaning-making" of the findings. Whatever specific form(s) the collaboration takes, the individuals involved should be carefully selected to include respected representatives of appropriate organizational divisions or units, governance and informal power structures (i.e., include the opinion-makers), faculty members or institutional researchers with recognized credentials in quantitative and qualitative research, and others whose visible involvement will lend weight to the goals and credibility of the assessment effort.

Visible, collaborative arrangements would, I believe, ameliorate a number of awareness and credibility problems. First, collaboration helps ensure that issues or circumstances in a broad array of campus organizational units will be taken into account when the overall program and specific studies are designed and when evidence is evaluated. Such cooperation helps ensure consideration of the interests and concerns of units and individuals most likely to be affected. Such representativeness would also promote community buy-in to assessment activities and reports.

Second, many first-year programs (or units dealing with first-year students) lack staff members with the breadth of research/evaluation training and experience required to do credible studies. Having such individuals (preferably faculty members from, say, sociology or psychology) involved would provide expert methodological guidance and advice to those doing the assessment and, thereby, promote credibility in the broader institutional community. Collaboration with a good writer from the institution's news staff (not public relations) is also likely to contribute to the readability of reports and to their accessibility to non-technical audiences.

Third, collaboration with relevant individuals and units in the review and discussion of assessment findings will help produce a more informed analysis of the meaning and implications of study findings. Such participation is another way to ensure community buy-in to the process and its results.

Fourth, collaborative efforts promote communication across organizational units and community constituencies. The more people involved in the development and interpretation phases of assessment, the greater the program or project's visibility in the community as a whole. A digression: Most assessment programs lack a carefully thought-out dissemination plan for converting findings into information and for getting that information into the hands of people who can act on it. It's sort of like dogs chasing cars: Most dogs have given no thought at all to what they'll do with the cars they catch. Turning data into useful information is a fine art with a number of dimensions, including format, length, language, content targeted to a specific audience, and knowledge of that audience's information needs. Collaboration with the users of assessment findings can help greatly in designing useful assessment reports. Dissemination plans should receive as much care, attention, and discussion as study designs.

Finally, collaborative efforts typically promote broader awareness, understanding, and appreciation of what other individuals and campus units do, the problems they confront, and how their activities relate to the goals and mission of the institution. Collaboration in assessment should contribute to a more "informed environment." In doing so, collaboration will help campus community members to appreciate the wide array of influences and experiences that shape student growth and to view students and institutions as complex entities that require coordinated, collaborative action to promote student learning effectively. Collaboration will, I believe, help all of us achieve the perspective John Gardner hopes to produce: to see the forest, as well as the trees.

Spurring Our Professional Curiosity about The First-Year Experience

Karl L. Schilling

As a child, I had a reputation for driving my parents, siblings, relatives, teachers, and innocent bystanders crazy by asking a lot of questions. I guess this inclination to ask questions, particularly questions that do not lend themselves to standard answers, may have led me to my work in assessment. After all, assessment is about asking hard questions that do not lend themselves to easy answers. As an unceasing "questioner" who has worked in higher education for 27 years, I have been most surprised by the lack of curiosity my colleagues, both faculty and administrators, have about students. They seem not very curious at all about whether those "things" we do with and for students have a significant impact—even though such things may absorb a lot of our time and energy. Why is there so little curiosity about the impact of our work with students?

Several years ago while doing a presentation at a graduate school of education, I speculated that faculty may not exercise much curiosity about the impact of "teaching and learning" efforts on students because most of us were really "amateurs" in this respect, having been trained primarily to do research and having never been really trained in pedagogy/teaching/learning.

In most other instances, college and university faculty are, by definition, experts. They know a great deal about their area of specialization. Yet, it is rare that this expertise extends to pedagogical practice. If college and university faculty began asking questions about student learning, they might quickly learn the limits of their expertise. So they abide by the dictum, "Don't ask, don't tell."

Nevertheless, as Karen Schilling and I (1998) argue in *Proclaiming and Sustaining Excellence: Assessment as a Faculty Role*, assessment is inherently, even quintessentially a scholarly act. Scholars work at asking good questions and then identifying methods for beginning to answer those questions with the understanding that a "definitive" answer will rarely be the result. Instead, we get better and better at asking the questions and developing ever more sophisticated ways for gathering evidence to assist in answering our questions. While acknowledging that we need to continue to learn more, we can begin to make changes as a result of the insights we have gained from our assessment efforts.

15

In this brief essay, I hope to provoke some questions related to the first-year experience. I have included a series of questions I posed to a higher education group in Virginia that I thought we ought to be able to answer about our impact on students, but which I suspect most of us could not.

Questions to Ask about the First-Year Experience

Pat Hutchings introduced the concept of getting "behind outcomes" in her 1998 AAHE monograph. She realized that knowing outcomes is at best a beginning. She argued we must get behind outcomes to look at the processes that produce these outcomes through innovative assessment approaches. Below, I offer a series of questions that would help us get behind outcomes if we could answer them. (The names in parenthesis are scholars who have noted the significance of each issue.) I will then provide an example of how this simple mode of investigating the student experience can provide new and helpful insights on the impact of our institutions.

1. What is the student experience of the institution? (Joe Katz)
2. What do faculty members know about learning theory, and how are they applying it in their classrooms? (Ted Marchese)
3. What does the student affairs staff know about learning theory, and how are they applying it in their work with students? (Ted Marchese)
4. Do faculty members know what happened in the classes that are prerequisite to the class they are teaching? (Karl Schilling)
5. How much time do students spend studying per week? How does use of time vary throughout the semester? Throughout the four years? (Karen and Karl Schilling, David Kalsbeek, and Richard Light)
6. Do you have a curriculum or just a set of courses? (Karen and Karl Schilling)
7. What metaphors would your students use to describe their experiences at your institution? (David Kalsbeek)
8. How are your students different after they spend four (or more) years with you? (Alexander Astin)
9. Is each student "known" by a faculty or staff person on campus? (Parker Palmer and William Willamon)
10. What rituals hold your campus together? (George Kuh)
11. What can you show prospective students about the kind and amount of work they will be doing in their first year? With what degree of specificity? (Karen and Karl Schilling)
12. How painful is the educational experience you offer your students? (Please do not confuse a painful education—meaning an educational experience that requires students to struggle with questions that don't have "right" answers—with an education that is a pain—meaning an educational experience that is full of meaningless busy work to get the "right" answer to questions that are not really meaningful.) (Douglas Heath and Karl Schilling)
13. Do you have a "culture of evidence" on your campus? (Ralph Wolfe)

Bonus Questions:
1. How are intellectual disagreements handled by students? By faculty? (Karl Schilling)
2. Are we making a difference? Are we making enough of a difference? (Daryl Krueger and Charles McClain)

3.   Were your first-year students given a job description? (Karen Schilling)

Making expectations explicit is the goal of this final question and can be facilitated by developing literal descriptions for the "job" of first-year student. I have included some job descriptions written by some of my colleagues in Virginia in response to the questions, "What is the job description for first-year students?" and "Do your first-year students have a clear "job description?" or "Are they on the job while clueless about their roles/expectations/responsibilities as a student?" You might find it interesting to ask your colleagues as well as your students for their job descriptions for first-year students. The resulting conversation may spark a larger discussion about answers to other questions regarding the student experience.

First-Year Job Descriptions

Wanted: Prospective Students Interested in Learning. The university is actively seeking a number of first-year students willing to take an active role in their own education. First-year students are responsible for basic self-management, including class attendance, completion of all assignments, and responsible decision making in all aspects of their college lives. Partnership with the university is encouraged in setting high standards, building solid successes, and aiming for a career after college that will benefit the student and society.

Successful students will have:
- ♦ Demonstrated ability to perform to high standards in high school
- ♦ Active interest in participating in their own education
- ♦ Active interest in expanding their minds and horizons
- ♦ Commitment to innovative approaches
- ♦ A balanced approach to liberal education and career preparation
- ♦ Willingness to take responsibility for learning
- ♦ Willingness to take responsibility for behaviors that advance or inhibit learning

During their first-year, students are expected to develop college-level skills in reasoning, communication, and technology that build a strong foundation for course work at the university as well as for their lives and careers after college. They also will pursue course work that helps them develop their ability to make ethical choices, appreciate beauty, understand the natural and social worlds in which they live, recognize the importance of the past, and work towards a better future.

The university is an Affirmative Action/Equal Opportunity university. Women, men, minorities, veterans, and persons with disabilities are encouraged to apply.

An entering first-year student must be willing to "accept" the following description of qualifications, duties, and attitudes requisite to success as a university student:

Academic responsibilities:
- ♦ Attend every class, be on time and in possession of proper materials, and be well prepared to engage in active learning

- ♦ Continuously improve in managing time, prioritizing commitments in terms of their relative importance to achieving academic goals
- ♦ Study two hours outside of class for every hour in class
- ♦ Visit professors during office hours to discuss course-specific strategies for succeeding and learning
- ♦ Continuously develop and strengthen academic study skills (e.g., notetaking, listening skills, oral communication, reading, writing, computation)
- ♦ Explore with faculty and advisors the purposes of higher education, especially in terms of how the opportunities provided through a university education relate to personal, social, and professional goals
- ♦ Set goals (academic, social, personal, and professional) that are concrete and measurable
- ♦ Research majors, careers, and relevant field experience and/or jobs
- ♦ Meet regularly with an academic advisor to plan the most appropriate program of study to meet the student's academic, social, personal, and professional goals
- ♦ Learn about campus academic support resources and how to use them effectively
- ♦ Learn to use the library, including the vast array of computer-based multimedia information resources available through the library and the Internet
- ♦ Continuously develop and/or enhance critical thinking and writing skills
- ♦ Continuously develop and/or enhance basic computing skills such as word processing and e-mail
- ♦ Understand and embrace the history and traditions of the university

Personal responsibilities:
- ♦ Develop an internal "locus of control"; learn to make informed decisions without inappropriate dependence on parental/family influences
- ♦ Develop personal relationships with peers and become a solid citizen within the university community
- ♦ Develop healthy communication patterns with family or other important non-university support people
- ♦ Become a fully engaged member of the campus community by attending campus events and participating in clubs and organizations
- ♦ Maintain physical and spiritual wellness
- ♦ Strengthen abilities to manage emotions
- ♦ Extend and deepen abilities to respect people from different cultures and people who have different lifestyles
- ♦ Strengthen abilities to manage personal finances
- ♦ Strengthen abilities to make healthy decisions with regard to alcohol and other substance use

First-Year Student Job Description (faculty perspective)

Academic Responsibilities—the person in this position will be expected to perform the following tasks to fulfill the ultimate goal of program completion (i.e., graduation) and future employment or further education:

- Attend 100% of classes
- Complete all assignments according to established timelines
- Be able to utilize appropriate computer software with 90% accuracy
- Develop a timeline for coursework completion consistent with established guidelines for satisfactory progress toward a degree
- Develop and implement a study schedule sufficient to maintain a minimum grade point average of 2.0 or greater

Social Responsibilities—the person in this position is expected to supplement his/her academic responsibilities with available and appropriate social responsibilities toward the ultimate goal of "education of the whole person." To this end he/she will:

- Assume a minimum of one leadership position within the university community during the period of residence
- Be able to exhibit the ability to work and live effectively in a diverse environment
- Be able to exhibit the ability to work effectively as part of a team
- Be able to exhibit the ability to learn to adapt in an environment of change

Personal Responsibilities—the person in this position is expected to conduct his/her personal life consistent with the established and acceptable policies and procedures of the university community. To this end he/she will:

- Agree to abide by the University Undergraduate Honor System
- Be responsible and ethical
- Exhibit some means of tangible contact with parent or guardian a minimum of once per academic term
- Abide by local, state and federal laws regarding the use of alcohol and drugs
- Be responsible for and practice all university policies and procedures

First-Year Student Job Description (upperclass peer perspective)

Academic Responsibilities—the person in this position will be expected to perform the following tasks to fulfill the ultimate goal of completing the career objective:

- Attend a majority of assigned classes
- Complete all instructor-assigned work in courses of your major
- Be 99% competent in the use of computer software appropriate to your career objectives
- Expect to take no more than 5 years to complete a four-year career objective and a similar ratio of time-to-task completion for other career objectives
- Be able to achieve a minimum grade point average every semester of not less than 2.0 to prevent any need for catch-up
- Prepare for the ultimate goal: to get a job

Social Responsibilities—the person in this position is expected to develop and cultivate an active social life to develop fully as an educated person. To this end he/she will:

- Participate in a minimum of one extracurricular activity each week (e.g., appreciation for the arts)
- Engage in at least one social activity weekly to help develop leadership skills
- Exhibit engagement with a group of students who possess compatible social values
- Engage in some form of service learning opportunity during the course of enrollment
- Be able to interact constructively with others

Personal Responsibilities—the person in this position is expected to conduct his/her personal life consistent with the established policies and procedures of the university community. To this end he/she will:

- Agree to abide by the University Undergraduate Honor System
- Exhibit the ability to treat others responsibly and ethically
- Abide by local, state and federal laws regarding the use of alcohol and drugs

References

Schilling, K. M., & Schilling, K. (1998). Proclaiming and sustaining excellence. *ASHE/ERIC Higher Education Series, 26*(3). San Francisco: Jossey-Bass/Wiley.

Assessing the First Year at a Community College

Trudy Bers

Three of the most formidable challenges to assessment in community colleges are:

1. Identifying and then "capturing" for assessment students who have completed a significant enough amount of course work at the community college to warrant the assumption the institution has had the opportunity to "affect" them
2. Differentiating the impact of the college from the impact of other agencies and experiences, especially employment, that have contributed to student learning
3. Examining "the first year" from the perspective of student expectations and realities

Why are these challenges so pervasive and so difficult to overcome in community colleges? Consider this question. What is the first-year experience at a community college or at any college, for that matter, with an open admissions policy where most or all students commute; live at home; attend school part-time; work part-time, if not full-time; and require remedial coursework in mathematics, reading, and/or composition? The idyllic nature of the first college year—presented in many textbooks and college promotions; mythologized by parents, legislators, and the media; and desired by faculty and staff—does not represent the experience of community college students, even those just out of high school. Why?

- ◆ Community college students do not live on campus where they socialize regularly with others of their own age who are also living away from home for the first time. Opportunities to learn from peers outside of class are limited as students disperse from campus when classes are over.
- ◆ Being a "student" is typically not the way in which community college students first identify themselves—"student" is not their full-time or often their primary "job." Indeed, their first obligation may be to work or family rather than to school.
- ◆ Many community college students spend a relatively short period of time at the institution, accumulating

less than a semester of credits and extending attendance over many semesters.

♦ Attending the local community college is for many an easy decision, even a "non-decision," because the non-school aspects of their lives—residence, friends, family obligations, jobs, social lives, and routines—can remain fixed.

♦ Like many of their counterparts at four-year schools, many community college students are unsure of what they want to be or even why they are in school.

♦ Also like many of their counterparts at four-year schools, community college students often lack knowledge about the education and skills needed to obtain and succeed in jobs in the career field they think is for them. There is simply a mismatch between their aspirations and expectations and the reality of their academic competencies and experiences—at least when they enter college. This is exacerbated by the fact that many have unrealistic perceptions of their skills, thinking their competencies are at higher levels than is actually the case.

If this seems like a particularly negative portrait of students spending their first college year at a community college, it is nonetheless accurate for many students. And these characteristics make assessing the first-year experience a substantial challenge in community colleges.

So, what are some ideas about how one might meet the challenge of assessing the first-year experience at the community college level?

1. Pay careful attention to Peter Ewell's excellent advice, elsewhere in this collection, to inventory and take advantage of information you already have about students. Consider identifying a sample of students for which data are gathered into a longitudinal database with variables derived not only from the student system, but also from surveys and other student-specific contacts. Though the universe of students will not be assessed in this approach, the result will most likely be a manageable and rich complement to census-based studies.

2. Acknowledge what Cliff Adelman (1992) has so aptly noted, that community colleges frequently play an "occasional" function in students' lives, serving their ad hoc and immediate needs. Thus, assessment will necessarily and appropriately take place at the course or course-cluster level rather than spanning a more traditional "first year." It also means that for many community college students the "first year" will comprise a selection of courses that meet immediate needs rather than a traditional general education curriculum.

3. Put together a team to design and collaborate on a first-year assessment study in which representatives from a variety of college offices identify what they would find valuable to know about their students. Pool resources to gather data and information, and meet together to interpret and discuss findings. Through the project, participants are likely to learn more about what their various offices do to provide instruction and services to first-year students while generating ideas for improvements. Assessment, in this approach, is the catalyst for conversation and improvement rather than simply the reporting of findings. Clearly, one of the strongest reasons for collaboration is the need I perceive to leverage expertise and resources so that

those without the technical skills or the office support to undertake assessment projects can still be participants at the assessment table.

4. Consider defining "the freshman year" from a multi-institutional rather than single-institution perspective. Form partnerships with researchers from other institutions from which large numbers of your students transfer or that receive students from your college. Share data—even the Family Educational Rights and Privacy Act (FERPA) will allow selected sharing for research purposes—and consider co-sponsoring focus groups, surveys, or other projects that gather students' insights about their first-year experiences regardless of where those experiences took place.

If there is a single theme in these comments it is that in community colleges, assessing the first-year experience must adapt to the realities of students and not be constrained by more traditional definitions of what constitutes "a first-year student" or "the first year."

Reference

Adelman, C. (1992). *The way we are: The community college as American thermometer*. Washington, DC: U. S. Department of Education.

Part 2

Methods & Tools for Assessment

Assessment of The First-Year Experience:
Six Significant Questions[1]

Joseph B. Cuseo

Rudyard Kipling once penned the following poetic adage: "I keep six honest serving men. They taught me all I knew. Their names are what & why and when & where and how & who." These half-dozen queries might serve as a useful framework for organizing assessment practices in the first year. While not all of Kipling's questions have profound theoretical significance, they all do have *practical* significance—which is very important to those of us who are working "in the trenches" to improve the educational experience of first-year students.

Assessment Question #1. Why?

This question refers to the purpose of assessment; it is the first question that needs to be addressed because its answer should guide and drive decisions relating to all other assessment questions.

When answering this question, the classic distinction between "formative" and "summative" assessment (Scriven, 1967) is an important one to keep in mind. If the purpose of assessment is formative, its goal is to obtain information that can be used as feedback to improve or fine-tune an existing program. In contrast, summative assessment is designed to "sum up" a program's overall value or impact—for the purpose of making bottom-line decisions about its adoption, retention, or expansion. The institutional assessment movement has been dominated by practices designed to meet accreditation standards that focus on the improvement or fine-tuning of traditional, well-established programs. Many first-year programs lack this long history of existence or acceptance; thus first-year experience assessment efforts sometimes have to be designed more intentionally for summative purposes in order to generate the type of "value-added" evidence that will support adoption and survival of first-year programs. Key questions to ask during the design process include:

---

[1] *Editor's Note:* This is a condensed version of Cuseo's original remarks on assessment. The text of the entire piece can be accessed on the web site of The Policy Center on the First Year of College.

1. Which assessment outcomes will command the most attention from key decision makers who control resource allocations?
2. Which assessment methodologies will generate the most compelling evidence for the value-added impact of first-year programs?
3. How will the results of assessment be packaged, presented, and delivered so as to maximize their persuasive power?

Assessment Question #2. What?

There are two components to this question:

1. What are the intended outcomes of assessment?
2. What is the intended target (unit or level) of assessment?

These questions are important for first-year experience practitioners to pursue because they may be the ones that are most likely to attract and hold the attention of those administrators who control the resources necessary for the implementation and continuation of first-year experience programs.

Previous first-year experience assessment efforts have focused predominantly on academic performance indicators, particularly student retention and academic achievement. This is an understandable and viable practice because these outcomes can be easily measured (quantified) and because they address two common concerns of college administrators and faculty.

However, the vast majority of college mission statements and related institutional goals refer to intended student outcomes that are not strictly academic or cognitive in nature (Kuh, Shedd, & Whitt, 1987; Lenning, 1988; Astin, 1991). Future first-year assessment efforts intentionally designed to demonstrate program impact on these broader outcomes of holistic development could fill a valuable void in the assessment literature. The viability of this form of first-year program assessment is promising because first-year initiatives have often been spearheaded by student development professionals, who tend to be more conversant with "noncognitive" (holistic) goals of student learning and development than are discipline-based, content-centered faculty. The presence of the student development perspective in many first-year programs brings an appreciation for the development of the "whole person" and a pursuit of educational goals that are strikingly compatible with college mission and goal statements. First-year experience assessment efforts that capitalize on this fortuitous compatibility between first-year experience program goals and mission-driven institutional goals can document that first-year experience programs are successfully fulfilling the college mission.

With respect to the second "what" question for assessment (What is the targeted unit or level of assessment?), potential assessment targets could be said to fall on a continuum ranging from "micro" to "macro" levels/units, such as individual, course, department, program, and institution.

As Astin (1991) suggests, within a college or university, many "subenvironments" exist which can affect institutional and first-year experience outcomes. Identifying those important subenvironments or component experiences of the total first-year experience is a first step in assessing how these components combine to affect end-of-first-year outcomes. Some of these subenvironments include new-student orientation, academic advisement, classroom instruction, the curriculum, the cocurriculum, academic support programs, and psychosocial support programs.

A look at these general subenvironments immediately suggests that there are additional sub-experiences nested within each one of them. Moreover, each of these seven subenvironments may be assessed with respect to the content of the program, the program organization, and the manner of program delivery.

Assessment Question #3. When?

This question refers to the timing of assessment, or more accurately, the timing of assessments because it is clear that a one-time, outcomes-only assessment will not provide useful information for assessing program impact or making program improvements. As Terenzini and Upcaft (1996) advise, "It is not enough to know simply whether change occurs; we must know when it occurs and why it occurs. These requirements suggest the need for several collections throughout the college career of an entering cohort of students" (pp. 221-22).

As an initial stab at implementing this recommendation, I offer the following taxonomy of data collection points for consideration.

Data-Collection Point #1. College Entry (Beginning of the First Year)

Data collected at this point can provide a baseline or pre-test needed for making meaningful comparisons with and interpretations of outcome data. College-entry assessment also provides a vehicle for understanding who our students are when they enter our doors. With this knowledge in mind, we can design our first-year teaching and educational programming more intentionally.

Data-Collection Point #2. End of the First Year

Another key data-collection point is the end of the first year. Assessment at the end of the first year might be useful for detecting the differential experiences or perceptions of those students who intend to return for their sophomore year versus those who do not. Also, accumulating evidence suggests that the first year of college may be a critical period for student learning and cognitive development. For instance, two independent studies conducted by the Washington Center for Improving the Quality of Undergraduate Education have revealed that more cognitive growth occurs during the first year than during any other year in the college experience (MacGregor, 1991). If we can replicate these findings through systematic, longitudinal assessment demonstrating that the undergraduate student "learning curve" accelerates most rapidly during the first year of college, this could provide potent empirical ammunition for first-year advocates.

Data-Collection Point #3. End of Sophomore Year/Beginning of Junior Year

Admittedly, this assessment point takes us beyond the first-year experience. However, I mention it because it may provide an important intermediate point for assessing the college experience. In particular, assessment at this point in the college experience may serve to diagnose the academic readiness of students for upper-division course work, junior transfers from two-year institutions, and the impact of general education course work.

Data-Collection Point #4. End of Senior Year

The senior year is an important transitional experience that represents the culmination of a college education. As such, it provides an opportunity for assessing the potential long-term impact of first-year programs by measuring their durability throughout the remaining years of college.

Historically, first-year program assessment has focused heavily on immediate or intermediate goals (e.g., retention through the first semester or first year). A useful direction for future assessments of first-year programs might be to explore their impact on broader, long-term student outcomes assessed at the end of the senior year.

Assessment Question #4. Who?

This question refers to the persons who may be involved in the assessment process; it embraces two component questions: (a) Who will the assessor(s) be? and (b) From whom will assessment data be collected?

Who Will the Assessor(s) Be?

Regarding the first question, an almost axiomatic answer is to have someone who is not associated with the first-year program being evaluated and who has no vested interested in its outcome conduct the assessment. This practice guards against charges of "evaluator bias"—the tendency of the person who designs or conducts the study to skew the findings unwittingly in the direction of its intended (hoped for) outcome. The use of an external evaluator is recommended for the assessment of any first-year program because it may serve to enhance the credibility of the findings, as well as their potential for commanding attention and promoting change.

From Whom Will Assessment Data Be Collected?

In terms of the second "who" question—from whom will assessment data be collected—students, alumni, faculty, student development professionals, administrators, administrative/staff assistants, and trustees are potential sources of information.

Naturally, since the first-year experience is a student-centered movement, students have been and are likely to continue to be the primary focus for first-year assessment. However, the undergraduate student population is not a homogeneous entity; it is composed of many subpopulations which differ in age, gender, race/ethnicity, residential status, national citizenship, admissions status, enrollment status, academic-decision status (e.g., declared versus undeclared major), level of educational aspiration, and employment status.

The impact of any educational intervention may vary for these different student subpopulations, resulting in "conditional" effects or "interactions" which may be masked if assessment data are simply aggregated and collapsed into a singular "average" measure. Thus, first-year experience assessment efforts should examine the differential effects of its programs on various student subpopulations.

Assessment of non-student populations (e.g., faculty, administration, staff) can allow for comparisons between their responses and those of students. Significant discrepancies or "gaps" emerging between the responses of students and non-students often have the potential to create a sense of cognitive "disequilibrium" or "dissonance" among college decision-makers which could provide the impetus for initiating administrative action on behalf of first-year students.

Assessment Question #5. Where?

This question refers to the location of data collection—i.e., Where will data be collected for use in the assessment process? To answer this question, it might be useful to organize the potential location points for data collection into several categories, such as office-use data, classroom-based/course-embedded data, and student program/service-use data.

With respect to the first category, elsewhere is this collection, Peter Ewell contends that a "data audit" is a valuable first step in the assessment process. Campus offices housing data that may be particularly relevant to first-year student assessment include those responsible for college admissions, new-student orientation, student placement testing, and Cooperative Institutional Research Program (CIRP) administration.

In regard to the second category, student program/service-use data, Lee Upcraft and John Schuh, also in this volume, recommend "keeping track of who participates in first-year year student programs." These student "footprints" (as Ewell calls them) may be tracked via (a) logs kept by student-service providers, (b) trace audits, a.k.a., "credit-card measures" of student involvement (e.g., using student identification cards to assess frequency of library use), (c) transcript analysis of course-enrollment patterns, and (d) "student development" or "cocurricular" transcripts of individual students' out-of-class participation.

With respect to classroom-based (course-embedded) assessment, student "course products" or "curricular artifacts" (as Karl Schilling calls them) may provide useful assessment data. Such products or artifacts would include students' written products and videotapes of student presentations or performances.

Assessment Question #6. How?

This question refers to how the assessment data will be collected, analyzed, and summarized— i.e., the research design or methodology to be used.

A comprehensive and well-balanced assessment of the first-year experience should include a complementary combination of different quantitative methods, and also qualitative methods, such as those described below in the following taxonomy.

Quantitative Methods
Pre-Test/Post-Test Design. This quantitative method is designed to assess the amount of student change between the onset and completion of an intervention program. The procedure involves administering an assessment instrument before program participation (pre-test) against which their post-program (post-test) responses can be compared.
Experimental Design. This research method involves comparing student outcomes for first-year students who are randomly assigned to either one of the following two groups: (a) an "experimental" group of students who participate in the program or (b) a "control" group of students who do not participate in the program.

Historically, this method has been considered to be the scientifically ideal or "true" experimental design for evaluating educational programs because it ensures randomized assignment of students to both the experimental and control groups (i.e., each student selected has an equal and independent chance of being placed into either of these groups). This design is ideal for guarding against the "volunteer effect" or "self-selection bias."

The major disadvantage of the experimental design is an ethical one: Its random selection of students to become program participants or non-participants (members of the control group) results in the arbitrary denial of program access to one-half of the students who want to become involved in the program and who are likely to benefit from it (Pascarella, 1986).

Quasi-Experimental Design. This research method involves comparing outcomes for first-year students who volunteer to participate in a program (experimental group) relative to a "matched" control group (i.e., selected first-year students who have elected not to participate in the program but whose personal characteristics are similar to or "match" the experimental group on important student variables that may influence the outcomes being measured). For example, in previously conducted first-year assessments, students in experimental and control groups have been matched with respect to such characteristics as (a) high school grade-point average; (b) standardized college-admission test scores; (c) predicted GPA; (d) residential or commuter status; and (e) demographic characteristics such as age, gender, race, or ethnicity. Matching program participants with non-participants in this fashion serves to control for, or rule out, the possibility that differences in student outcomes associated with program participation could be due to the fact that program participants had personal characteristics which differed significantly from non-participants.

Time-Series Design. In this research design, outcomes assessed after implementation of the first-year program are compared with the outcomes achieved prior to the program's implementation. For example, first year-to-sophomore retention rates at the college after adoption of a first-year seminar are compared with first year-to-sophomore retention rates for the years preceding course adoption.

The advantage of this design is that it provides a type of "historical" control group—against which the effects of program participation may be compared—without having to withhold the program from a portion of entering first-year students so they can serve as a "contemporary" control group.

However, two caveats must be issued with respect to the time-series research design. First, the personal characteristics of entering first-year students during years before and after implementation of the first-year program should be similar or matched so that any changes in student outcomes subsequent to program implementation cannot simply be due to historical changes in the entry characteristics of the first-year class. Second, two or more years of outcome data should be gathered before and after institutional initiation of the program in order to compare pre- and post-program outcomes—not just the year immediately before and after program implementation—because any year-to-year fluctuations in student outcomes (e.g., retention) may simply be due to random chance deviation (Pascarella, 1986).

Multiple Regression Analysis (a.k.a., Multivariate Analysis). In short, multiple regression analysis involves computing correlations between student-outcome variables (e.g., student retention or academic performance) and two other types of variables: (a) student input variables (e.g., entering students' SAT scores) and (b) college experience variables (e.g., student participation in a particular first-year program). To illustrate, if students who participate in a first-year experience program (e.g., freshman seminar) are retained at a higher-than-expected rate based on their student input (college-entry) characteristics, then this difference suggests that participating in the program (a college experience variable) is having a positive effect on student retention (student outcome variable). It might be said that multiple regression analysis attempts to control for confounding student variables statistically (i.e., by computing correlations between student input variables and outcomes), whereas the aforementioned experimental and quasi-experimental research designs attempt to gain this control procedurally (i.e., by the procedures used to select and assign students to experimental and control groups). For a more detailed explanation of multiple regression analysis, consult the appendices in Astin (1991) or Pascarella and Terenzini (1991).

Qualitative Research Methods

Qualitative data take the form of human actions and words (e.g., students' written or verbal comments), and they are analyzed by means of "human instruments" (Kuh, Schuh, Whitt, & Associates, 1991, p. 273). Also, in contrast to the hypothesis testing and scientific methodology that characterizes quantitative research, qualitative research is "exploratory [and] inductive, . . . one does not manipulate variables or administer a treatment. What one does is observe, intuit, [and] sense what is occurring in natural settings" (Merriam, 1988, p. 17). Two typical qualitative methodologies are text analyses and convening of focus groups.

Analysis of Students' Written Comments. Written comments made on student surveys can provide a good source of qualitative data. These comments may be difficult to summarize and manipulate statistically, but they have the potential for providing poignant, in-depth information on program strengths and weaknesses, as well as providing an index of students' subjective feelings about the program.

Historically, surveys and questionnaires have not been considered to be qualitative research methods because they generate quantitative data (numerical ratings). However, written comments made by respondents to clarify their ratings do represent legitimate qualitative data, the content of which can be analyzed and classified systematically. Even the sheer number of positive or negative written responses students make beneath a specific item on a rating survey may itself serve as a measure of the importance or intensity of student feelings about the issue addressed by that item.

Focus Groups. Succinctly defined, a focus group is a small (6 to 12 person) group that meets with a trained moderator in a relaxed environment to discuss a selected topic or issue, with the goal of eliciting participants' perceptions, attitudes, and ideas (Bers, 1989). In contrast to surveys or questionnaires that solicit individual students' written comments, focus-group interviews solicit students' verbal responses in a discussion-group setting. Verbal responses to questions often turn out to be more elaborate and extensive than written comments, and they may reveal underlying beliefs or assumptions that are not amenable to behavioral observation (Reinharz, 1993).

Conclusion

While those assessing the first-year experience will seek to answer all six of these questions, the question of "how" is in some ways the most crucial. Moreover, assessment designers may find that a single answer to this question is inadequate. In fact, it is almost axiomatic among program-evaluation scholars that the use of "multiple measures" represents a more reliable and valid procedure than exclusive reliance on a single research method or data source (Wergin, 1988). Including multiple measures in the assessment plan for first-year programs increases the likelihood that subtle differences in the effects of the program will be detected. Use of multiple methods also can be used to demonstrate a consistent pattern of results across different methods—a cross-validation procedure known in the assessment literature as "triangulation" (Fetterman, 1991) or "convergent validity" (Campbell

& Fiske, 1959). Such cross-validation serves to minimize the likelihood that the results obtained are merely an artifact of any one single method used to obtain them, and it magnifies the persuasive power of the results obtained so that they be used more effectively to convert first-year experience-program skeptics.

References

Astin, A. W. (1991). *Assessment for excellence: The philosophy and practice of assessment and evaluation in higher education*. New York: Macmillan.

Bers, T. H. (1989). The popularity and problems of focus-group research. *College & University, 64*(3), 260-268.

Campbell, D. T., & Fiske, D. W. (1959). Convergent and discriminant validation by the multitrait-multimethod matrix. *Psychological Bulletin, 56*, 81-105.

Fetterman, D. M. (1991). Auditing as institutional research: A qualitative focus. In D. M. Fetterman (Ed.), Using qualitative methods in institutional research (pp. 23-34). *New Directions for Institutional Research, 72*. San Francisco: Jossey-Bass.

Kuh, G., Schuh, J., Whitt, E., & Associates (1991). *Involving colleges*. San Francisco: Jossey-Bass.

Kuh, G., Shedd, J., & Whitt, E. (1987). Student affairs and liberal education: Unrecognized (and unappreciated) common law partners. *Journal of College Student Personnel, 28*(3), 252-260.

Lenning, O. T. (1988). Use of noncognitive measures in assessment. In T. W. Banta (Ed.), Implementing outcomes assessment: Promise and perils (pp. 41-52). *New Directions for Institutional Research, 50*. San Francisco: Jossey-Bass.

MacGregor, J. (1991). What differences do learning communities make? *Washington Center News, 6*(1), pp. 4-9.

Merriam, S. B. (1988). *Case study research in education: A qualitative approach*. San Francisco: Jossey-Bass.

Pascarella, E. T. (1986). A program for research and policy on student persistence at the institutional level. *Journal of College Student Personnel, 27*(2), 100-107.

Pascarella, E. T., & Terenzini, P. T. (1991). *How college affects students: Findings and insights from twenty years of research*. San Francisco: Jossey-Bass.

Reinharz, S. (1993). *On becoming a social scientist*. New Brunswick, NJ: Transaction Publishers.

Scriven, M. (1967). The methodology of evaluation. *Perspectives of curriculum evaluation, AERA monograph series on curriculum evaluation, 1*. Chicago: Rand McNally & Co.

Terenzini, P. T., & Upcraft, M. L. (1996). Assessing program and service outcomes. In M. L. Upcraft & J. H. Schuh (Eds.), *Assessment in student affairs: A guide for practitioners* (pp. 217-239). San Francisco: Jossey-Bass.

Wergin, J. F. (1988). Basic issues and principles in classroom assessment. In J. H. McMillan (Ed.), Assessing students' learning (pp. 5-17). *New Directions for Teaching and Learning, 34*. San Francisco: Jossey-Bass.

Assessment Resources on the Web

Randy L. Swing

Author's Note:

In his posting to the FYA-List, Ephraim Schechter introduced readers to the meta-collection of assessment information known as the Internet Resources for Higher Education Outcomes Assessment, which is part of North Carolina State University's assessment web site. Schechter produced an online guided tour of the web site that encouraged FYA-List members to explore the range of assessment information available with just a few computer mouse clicks.

We cannot freeze the Internet or easily transform Schechter's guided tour into a print form; however, we can build on this earlier contribution by exploring key web resources on assessment topics. This essay is not intended to provide an in depth examination of the Internet Resources for Higher Education Outcomes Assessment web site. Readers should visit http://www2.acs.ncsu.edu/ UPA/assmt/resource.htm (address as of July 2001) to explore this topic further. Because the resources listed on this web site are housed on university and college web servers across the country, they should be easily accessible to future readers via an Internet search engine even if Schechter's web site itself is no longer available

The following essay builds on Schechter's original posting to the FYA-List. I am indebted to him for providing the foundation for this article and for his work of collecting, categorizing, and evaluating online assessment material—an effort that has significantly advanced higher education assessment practice.

Randy L. Swing

The higher education assessment movement came of age along with the rise of the World Wide Web, so it is not surprising that much of the foundational work in assessment is available on the Internet. The Web quickly became a powerful link between practitioners who shared assessment tools and techniques in a period when there was little guidance available in print sources. Moreover, the speed of change in this field is too rapid to depend heavily on print materials, so the Web continues to serve a vital role in higher education assessment. The Web allows almost immediate updates on new assessment tools and strategies and provides an easily accessible training ground for those entering the field. Two examples are particularly cogent. First, in the past five years a number of new assessment instruments have been created, and all were launched with announcements over the Internet. Second, many higher educators have little formal training in outcomes assessment and have developed their skills using online resources and opportunities for exchanging ideas with colleagues. Thus, the Web has played a major role in enhancing the professional skills needed by many higher educators with assessment duties and is likely to continue as an influential medium for advancing assessment practice. In this article two of the major sources of assessment information and exchange—listservs and meta-lists—are reviewed.

Listservs

Building on a strong tradition of sharing with each other, institutional researchers and first-year program administrators have developed a number of Internet-based communication methods. The listserv, one such method, is an e-mail distribution list composed of subscribers who share a common interest. Assessment listserv members use the electronic medium to ask questions, exchange ideas, and swap news about new assessment tools and techniques. Because news travels more rapidly through listservs than through traditional print forms, listservs provide essential communication about hot topics and new opportunities.

One of the great advantages of listserv communication is that questions posted often are answered within minutes or hours, significantly reducing the amount of time needed to gather information through traditional methods. The other great advantage is that lists often contain a wide range of perspectives and frequently have members with very specific expertise. It is common for expert assessment professionals to provide support to those with less assessment expertise.

Listservs should not be confused with refereed professional exchanges such as the scholarship in print and in some online journals. Fortunately, the public nature of the listserv often provides a peer review function, safeguarding against misinformation. Because all list members view responses posted to the list, exchanges frequently generate alternative opinions, refinements, or contradictions. Any controversial opinion expressed on a listserv is likely to create a lively discussion and exchange of opinions.

Assessment listservs provide an important contribution in a field that is changing rapidly by providing announcements about conferences, new books, new surveys, and other "hot" developments. Some listservs allow announcement of for-profit products and services; however, most restrict postings to non-profit organizations or third-party announcements. Listserv membership may result in some unwanted e-mail, but having access to the latest breaking news and to some of the best thinkers in the field offsets this disadvantage.

Three listservs are of greatest interest to first-year assessment practitioners. Below are brief descriptions of ASSESS-L, CAPS, and FYA-List.

ASSESS-L, hosted by the University of Kentucky, is an open list of general discussion about higher-education assessment. The list has been active for nearly 10 years under the supervision of Roseanne Hogan and the assessment office at the University of Kentucky. Subscribers include a wide variety of academic administrators and faculty. The list had a membership of 747 people in July 2001. First-year assessment topics are often posted; however, ASSESS-L does not focus primarily on this part of the higher education experience. In past years ASSESS-L frequently provided educators with the first announcements of new assessment instruments, opportunities to participate in pilot studies, and other information about the changing assessment landscape.

The Consortium for Assessment and Planning Support (CAPS) is a list open only to CAPS members (in 2001 membership cost was $15.00/year). CAPS members include higher educators with direct responsibility in assessment and/or strategic planning. Members gather annually for conferences where they meet face-to-face. The CAPS list was established in 1998 by Larry Kelley at the University of Louisiana at Monroe and is hosted by Heather Langdon at Appalachian State University. Currently some 350 people subscribe to the list. CAPS members use the list to share information about campus-based assessment efforts. A number of consortia projects have been formed as CAPS colleagues develop multi-institutional assessment efforts. In recent years, large projects assessing learning communities and general education outcomes have developed out of this listserv.

The First-Year Assessment List (FYA-List) was created in 2000 by staff at the Policy Center on the First Year of College with the support of The Atlantic Philanthropies and The Pew Charitable Trusts. This list, originally monitored by Randy Swing, is dedicated to issues of assessing first-year students or first-college-year programs and is hosted by the National Resource Center for The First-Year Experience and Students in Transition at the University of South Carolina. Enrollment is open to any interested individual. In addition to general messages contributed by members, FYA-List includes invited essays contributed by assessment experts. Themes include survey instruments, qualitative research, assessment structures, and more. The unique feature of FYA-List is that it focuses on assessment of the first college year. Essays are archived for ease of retrieval and formatted for easy printing. In summer 2001, the list had more than 815 members, making it the largest assessment-focused listserv on the Web.

Meta-list Web Sites

A second form of Internet information is the meta-list. A meta-list web site is an organized collection of links to other web-based information. While a search engine and patience would uncover the links listed in a meta-list, these sites are more useful than individual efforts because content has been screened by the site owner and organized for easy searching.

The most noted meta-list on the topic of assessment is the Internet Resources for Higher Education Outcomes Assessment created by Ephraim Schechter in 1995 at the University of Colorado - Boulder. The list was enhanced while Schechter served as assessment officer at the University of North Carolina General Administration and developed further when he and the list moved to North Carolina State University in 1998. This extensive collection of URLs includes links to handbooks, philosophical statements, listservs, assessment web sites (individuals', universities', and organizations') and assessment resources. Particularly important is the organization that Schechter provides. Links are listed in categories and contain brief synopses, allowing users to locate information quickly on a wide array of assessment topics.

On this web site, for example, one can find:

♦ The AAHE Principles of Good Practice in Assessment and other documents related to assessment practice

- ♦ Examples of institutional assessment policies, plans, and assessment data collection forms
- ♦ Institutional assessment reports showing findings and methods of reporting results
- ♦ Institutional "handbooks" for faculty and administrators designing and implementing assessment plans
- ♦ Examples of assessment surveys, tests, and questionnaires
- ♦ Information about assessment techniques—from statistical modeling to focus group methods
- ♦ A bibliography of assessment resources

The combination of a wide range of assessment information and the organization system provided by the site manager makes a good meta-list user friendly and valuable for repeat visits. Even the best maintained meta-list will contain some inactive links as referenced web pages are deleted or moved without notice. The wide range of free information available to the reader offsets the occasional broken link.

Summary

Listservs and meta-lists are two important sources for information about assessing the first college year available via the World Wide Web. These should be considered, along with print materials and conferences, as key resources for the professional development of higher educators charged with assessing the first college year.

Developmental Theory as a Basis for Assessment

Nancy J. Evans

The rallying call for administrators everywhere seems to be "We need more assessment!" Determining what factors to assess, though, is often a challenge for evaluators. Administrators want evidence that programs are achieving positive outcomes yet they rarely delineate what those outcomes should be. Evaluators are left to their own devices to determine what will satisfy their superiors. Given the ambiguity of the situation and frequently tight timelines for preparing reports, it is tempting to report data that are readily available and easily summarized. Unfortunately, easily collected data rarely provide an accurate or complete picture of the extent to which learning outcomes have truly been achieved. Retention rates, for example, are commonly included in assessments of academic programs. While retention data provide some information on satisfaction and academic success, they do little to provide a comprehensive picture of even these outcomes since students may stay in school even when they are unhappy; and satisfied, successful students leave school for reasons beyond their control. GPA, another common measure of academic success, is also limited because it reveals little about what a student actually gained from a particular class or academic program.

The impact of out-of-class experiences, in particular, is rarely examined. Yet institutional mission statements usually stress the importance of preparing well-rounded, ethical citizens who understand themselves, the needs of those around them, and the larger issues facing society. These goals are often addressed in settings outside the classroom. Examining the impact of activities that complement in-class learning, such as service learning, study abroad, learning communities, extended orientation programs, and involvement in student government and other student activities, is important in determining the extent to which college attendance results in the full range of knowledge, skills, and attitudes that colleges purport to develop.

Effective assessment plans require a clear delineation of what outcomes are being examined. To provide a truly comprehensive assessment of learning outcomes, educators need to consider how students might be different as a result of both their academic and out-of-class experiences. Developmental theory provides direction for such assessment, at

39

both the macro-level and with regard to specific programs and interventions. Developmental theory provides an overview of outcomes that educators can expect college to have on students in the areas of cognitive, interpersonal, and intrapersonal growth.

Over the last decade, developmental theory has expanded well beyond the "big three"—Chickering (1969), Perry (1968), and Kohlberg (1969). A great deal of attention has been paid to learning styles, identity development of diverse populations, and adult development, in particular. Research and theory investigating developmental issues, cognitive development, and moral development of women, adults, and multicultural populations have extended the work of Chickering, Perry, and Kohlberg (Evans, Forney, & Guido-DiBrito, 1998). Much of this theory is extremely useful in determining outcomes that might be expected in college. In this piece, I provide a brief description of several theories useful in assessment and discuss some specific strategies for using each to measure student growth or change. For a more complete overview of the student development literature, see Evans, Forney, and Guido-DiBrito (1998).

Cognitive Development

Cognitive structural theory is especially helpful in pinpointing outcomes that might be expected with regard to intellectual development throughout students' college careers. These theories focus on how people think, reason, and make meaning of their experiences. Cognitive development is viewed as a progression through stages that become increasingly complex. Perry (1968), Baxter Magolda (1992), and others suggest that students usually begin college thinking dualistically. Dualistic thinkers believe that there is one correct answer to every problem, and that teachers will supply these answers. They believe that their job as students is to absorb this information and to reproduce it on exams. As a result of exposure to cognitive conflict experienced when this approach is found to be inadequate, students come to see that there are not always "right" answers and that context often determines how problems are addressed. Teachers come to be viewed as guides who have knowledge that can be helpful in analyzing situations, but students will ultimately realize that individuals are responsible for coming to their own conclusions. This type of relativistic thinking is an important goal of a college education. Assessment of students' levels of cognitive development can be done using standardized assessment tools, such as Moore's (1989) Learning Environmental Preferences Measure. Another viable method is qualitative assessment consisting of interviews with selected students over time to determine if their thinking becomes more complex and relativistic as they progress through college. Examining students' writing for evidence of increased cognitive complexity is another option.

Another cognitive structural theory particularly applicable to assessment of academic outcomes is King and Kitchener's (1994) reflective judgment model. These authors focus on how people come to conclusions about "ill-structured problems"—those questions that have no apparent right answer, such as overpopulation, hunger, pollution, or inflation. Indeed, most problems facing society could be considered ill structured. Also a stage model, King and Kitchener's approach suggests that as students begin college, their thinking is often at a prereflective stage where they do not realize that a problem may not have an absolute answer. Students at this stage are unable to use evidence to determine a solution. With appropriate challenges, individuals move to a more advanced reflective stage in which they come to see that knowledge must be actively constructed and viewed within a particular context. At this level, individuals understand that decisions must be based on relevant data and that conclusions are always open to reconsideration if new information comes to light. King and Kitchener (1994) have developed the Reflective Judgment Interview to assess where individuals are with regard to the seven stages in their model. Although trained raters must score this instrument, it could be used in formal assessments of cognitive development. Subject-specific assessment tools might also be developed.

Learning Style

Learning style data can also be useful in assessments. Kolb (1984) suggests that students vary in the ways in which they absorb and process information. He notes four components that make up the learning cycle:

1. Concrete experience (CE) or direct engagement in learning activities
2. Reflective observation (RO) or consideration of those experiences from various perspectives
3. Abstract conceptualization (AC) or formation of ideas and views about the experiences
4. Active experimentation (AE) or using the new ideas

Concrete experience and abstract conceptualization form a grasping dimension while reflective observation and active experimentation form a processing dimension. Based on their preferences for one or the other of the two components associated with each dimension, students' learning styles can be determined. Accommodators (CE and AE) like action, solve problems through trial and error, and like to try new things. Divergers (CE and RO) are people- and feeling-focused, imaginative, and good at generating alternatives. Assimilators (AC and RO) focus on ideas and are good at theoretical reasoning and model building. Convergers (AC and AE) like technical tasks and excel at problem solving and decision making. The Learning Style Inventory (Kolb, 1985) can be used to assess learning styles. Evaluators might explore the impact of particular types of learning situations on students with different learning styles, the overall performance of students with different learning styles, or preferences of students with different learning styles for particular classes, majors, or instructors.

Moral Reasoning

The appropriate use of technology, genetic engineering, cloning, and the impact of medical advances are but a few of the moral dilemmas currently facing our society. Given these challenges, the moral and ethical development of students is a critical dimension for educators to address. Kohlberg (1984) and Gilligan (1993) provide guidance concerning the development of moral reasoning from (a) self-centered decision-making through (b) consideration of how others will view decisions to (c) a higher level of thinking based on principles. While Kohlberg's model stresses justice as the basis for moral decision-making, Gilligan emphasizes caring and connectedness. Both approaches can be useful for determining ways in which students approach moral and ethical dilemmas and the impact of coursework and programs designed to increase sensitivity to ethical and moral considerations.

Either standardized instruments, such as the Defining Issues Test (Rest, 1986), or qualitative interviewing could be used to assess the level of moral reasoning.

Identity Development

In an increasingly diverse society, racial and ethnic identity development becomes an important goal in higher education. Helping both white students and students of color develop a clear sense of who they are as racial and ethnic persons and learn to relate to individuals of different backgrounds effectively is a key to the cross-cultural communication necessary to work in a global society. The outcomes of programs and curricular initiatives designed with this purpose in mind can be assessed using appropriate measures of racial and ethnic identity. The work of Phinney (1990); Cross (1995); Helms and Cook (1999); Ponterotto, Casas, Suzuki, and Alexander (1995); and others should be consulted.

Adult Development

In addition to being more diverse with regard to race and ethnicity, the majority of students are no longer 18 to 22 years old. Adult development theory provides an understanding of the issues that students face across the life span. Nancy Schlossberg's transition theory (Schlossberg, Waters, & Goodman, 1995) provides a framework for delineating factors related to the transition, the individual, and the environment that are likely to impact how an individual will be affected by a given transition at a particular point in time. This framework can be a useful guide for determining how successfully a particular program or institution is assisting adult students enrolled in college. Since all students go through a variety of transitions during their college careers, this approach can also be used to assess the success with which traditional age students address changes.

Psychosocial Development

Finally, Chickering's theory of psychosocial development (Chickering & Reisser, 1993) is still very useful in determining appropriate interpersonal and intrapersonal outcomes of college. In the latest revision of this theory, Chickering and Reisser outline a series of seven developmental issues faced by college students, including developing competence, managing emotions, moving through autonomy toward interdependence, developing mature interpersonal relationships, establishing identity, developing purpose, and developing integrity. Student progress along each of these dimensions could be assessed over time to provide an overall picture of the impact of their college experience on their development. Programs and coursework could also be identified that would be likely to contribute to specific dimensions, and outcomes in these areas could be assessed. The Iowa Student Development Inventories (Hood, 1986) measure most of these dimensions and are easily administered.

In summary, knowledge and use of student development theory is a major asset when determining outcomes that can be expected from college. In turn, developmental outcomes provide an appropriate and meaningful basis for assessment of the impact of educational initiatives, both in and out of the classroom. Examination of such outcomes must not be neglected for the sake of expediency.

References

Baxter Magolda, M. B. (1992). *Knowing and reasoning in college: Gender-related patterns in students' intellectual development.* San Francisco: Jossey-Bass.

Chickering, A. W. (1969). *Education and identity.* San Francisco: Jossey-Bass.

Chickering, A. W., & Reisser, L. (1993). *Education and identity* (2nd ed.). San Francisco: Jossey-Bass.

Cross, W. E., Jr. (1995). The psychology of nigrescence: Revisiting the Cross model. In J. G. Ponterotto, J. M. Casas, L. A. Suzuki, & C. M. Alexander (Eds.), *Handbook of multicultural counseling* (pp. 93-122). Thousand Oaks, CA: Sage.

Evans, N. J., Forney, D. S., & Guido-DiBrito, F. (1998). *Student development in college.* San Francisco: Jossey-Bass.

Gilligan, C. (1993). *In a different voice: Psychological theory and women's development.* Cambridge, MA: Harvard University Press. (Original work published 1982)

Helms, J. E., & Cook, D. A. (1999). *Using race and culture in counseling and psychotherapy: Theory and process.* Needham Heights, MA: Allyn & Bacon.

Hood, A. B. (Ed.). (1986). *The Iowa Student Development Inventories.* Iowa City, IA: Hitech Press.

King, P. M., & Kitchener, K. S. (1994). *Developing reflective judgment: Understanding and promoting intellectual growth and critical thinking in adolescents and adults.* San Francisco: Jossey-Bass.

Kohlberg, L. (1969). Stage and sequence: The cognitive developmental approach to socialization. In D. A. Goslin (Ed.), *Handbook of socialization theory and research* (pp. 347-480). Chicago: Rand McNally.

Kohlberg, L. (1984). *Essays on moral development: Vol. II. The psychology of moral development.* San Francisco: Harper & Row.

Kolb, D. A. (1984). *Experiential learning: Experience as the source of learning and development.* Englewood Cliffs, NJ: Prentice Hall.

Kolb, D. A. (1985). *The learning style inventory.* Boston: McBer.

Moore, W. S. (1989). The learning environment preferences: Exploring the construct validity of an objective measure of the Perry scheme of intellectual development. *Journal of College Student Development, 30,* 504-514.

Perry, W. G., Jr. (1968). *Forms of intellectual and ethical development in the college years: A scheme.* New York: Holt, Rinehart & Winston.

Phinney, J. S. (1990). Ethnic identity in adolescents and adults: Review of research. *Psychological Bulletin, 108,* 499-514.

Ponterotto, J. G., Casas, J. M., Suzuki, L. A., & Alexander, C. M. (1995). *Handbook of multicultural counseling.* Thousand Oaks, CA: Sage.

Rest, J. R. (1986). *The defining issues test* (3rd ed.). Minneapolis: University of Minnesota, Center for the Study of Ethical Development.

Schlossberg, N. K., Waters, E. B., & Goodman, J. (1995). *Counseling adults in transition* (2nd ed.). New York: Springer.

Technology-Supported Assessment

Randy L. Swing

The remarks by John Gardner, Peter Ewell, Karl Schilling, Trudy Banta, and George Kuh elsewhere in this collection encourage us to think about (a) the first college year as a unit of analysis; (b) the way we organize data to facilitate longitudinal analysis; (c) the values which undergird our view of the first-year student; (d) the way we explore, interpret, and form action plans from assessment data; and (e) the opportunities arising from new assessment instruments. This article continues these themes by reviewing technologies to support our assessment of the first-year experiences of college students.

It must have been only a short leap from counting apples and bags of spices on the first abacus to using that technology for counting people and ideas. Today, we owe many of the advances in assessment and evaluation to technologies driven by computers. In the following essay, I comment on web-based surveys, scannable surveys, and technology-assisted focus groups—three technologies with great promise for supporting first-year assessment efforts.

Electronic Surveys on the World Wide Web

Collecting data using a web-based survey is a common practice in assessment offices and has been used in large data collections such as George Kuh's National Study of Student Engagement. While the jury is still deliberating the impact of this technology, early evidence suggests that web-based surveys effectively increase response rates, especially among males who are often underrepresented in traditional mail-back survey data.

Unlike response rates, other possible biases created by using web-based surveys are more difficult to identify. Will a high rate of response by technology-savvy students introduce a new form of bias to the data? Does the lack of control created by "any time and any place" data collection skew the data? Are web-based data subtly contaminated by some human/computer interaction? We are hardly out of the starting gate in using web-based surveys in collegiate assessment, and there are already numerous research questions awaiting exploration.

Even though methodological concerns exist, the mammoth advantages of web-based data collection make the technology an inviting option. Web-based surveys, especially when coupled with e-mail announcements and follow-up contacts, greatly reduce or eliminate postage and printing expenses—once a large consideration in assessment data collection. A second major advantage is that open-ended responses can be collected in databases without time-consuming and error-prone transcription. In addition, web-based surveys allow immediate access to data and expanded possibilities for follow-up with non-respondents.

Software, such as "Cold Fusion," automates the production of web-based surveys. In general the software for advanced production of these surveys is moderately expensive ($300 - $750) and requires a significant investment of time to master. It is possible for persons with a basic understanding of Hypertext Markup Language (HTML) to build simple forms in a text editor or to use web page design software such as Front Page and Netscape Composer to do these tasks. If the thought of designing a survey for the web makes you break out in a cold sweat, find a friend in the computer services area to help with your first survey. Much of the coding for future surveys is simply a matter of cutting the opening code from the first survey and pasting it into new surveys.

Scannable Paper Survey Forms

A second technology now available and affordable provides the ability to print and scan custom survey forms. The three key elements of this technology are (a) software to enable form development and printing, (b) an OMR (Optical Mark Recognition) scanner for processing completed survey forms, and (c) OMR software to enable the scanner to read and record data from the completed surveys. The software is not cheap ($550 – $1,900), and OMR scanners vary in price based on the number of sheets per minute they can process and whether they read one or two sides of the survey in a single pass (starting price $4,000). These are frequently sold as bundled packages. Scanning Dynamics' Form Shop and Bubble Shop, Scantron's Pulse Survey II and Survey Pro, and Principia's Remark Office OMR are examples of software for these tasks.

Early OMR technology used standardized pre-printed answer sheets and separate pages of survey questions. That format required the respondent to match question and answer numbers carefully across two sets of print materials—not always an easy task to perform. Additionally, the preprinted answer sheets restricted the range and type of responses available to the survey author. Even with these restrictions, the use of OMR grew rapidly because of the speed with which individual responses could be processed and the reduction of errors through the elimination manual data entry.

Current technology continues the advantages of the early OMR technology and provides important advances in survey form design. Researchers can combine question and answer scales on the same page and freely mix question formats (e.g., true/false, multiple choice) since both the question formats and answer scales are customizable.

Educators can quickly develop technical skill in using the software; however, survey form design, so that layouts do not confuse respondents or bias their answers, requires careful consideration and skill. It is tempting to reduce font size and stack items to minimize the number of pages to be printed and scanned while ignoring that adequate spacing and item placement are critical to developing an effective survey. Survey designers should conduct pilot administrations to ensure that respondents are not confused by the layout and do, in fact, answer questions in the order consistent with that envisioned by the survey designer.

Start-up costs for producing scannable surveys may seem expensive in "academic dollars," but this technology greatly expands data collection possibilities and data accuracy. Scanners and OMR software are accessible to average computer users today and can easily be an addition to the assessment toolbox.

Technology-Enhanced Focus Groups

Using focus groups to collect data about college student experiences and satisfaction can be a powerful assessment technique. Focus groups have traditionally been used in exploratory research and survey development as a first step toward understanding and narrowing a research topic and as a final research step to explore "why?" questions raised by analyzing other data forms. For example, data from print surveys or academic records might show some pattern of student behavior but not explain the underlying conditions associated with that behavior. Focus groups, especially when conducted by a skilled moderator, can produce rich insights as part of a coordinated assessment plan.

The literature on focus groups is replete with best practice strategies for sample selection, moderator behavior, physical setting, and data capture. Little has been written, however, about how computing technologies can improve focus group techniques. One form of technology assistance is the Perception Analyzer/Learning Analyzer by Columbia Information Systems. The technology components consist of (a) hand-held wireless or wired dials, (b) an interface for connection to a laptop computer, and (c) software for data collection, analysis, and display. PowerPoint software is used to combine and display questions, graphic images, videos, and other audio-visual materials; and participants' reactions are captured through the two-way communication between the hand-held dials and the moderator's computer. The captured data provides immediate feedback and is stored for future analyses. Some of the most exciting advantages of this technology include:

1. Each participant responds privately using his/her hand-held dial so that anonymity can be maintained. The individual dials allow minority or controversial opinions to be freely expressed and not overly influenced by others who might speak first, speak with great emotion, or speak from perceived power/status positions.

2. All participants are actively involved in a technology-assisted focus group and can "all speak at the same time" via the dials, thus allowing these focus groups to accommodate 30 to 100 participants easily and produce richer data—far eclipsing traditional focus group limitations of 8 to 12 participants. Combining technology-assisted sessions with breakout traditional sessions can provide powerful ways to screen and organize focus groups. Equally important is that participants—even reticent public speakers— find the technology fun to use, making it easy to stay focused, involved, and attentive.

3. Moderators can immediately assess statistical and graphic results (e.g., mean, standard deviation, calculated multi-question scores) to drill down into

specific areas by shaping the focus group on the fly. Just as important, the use of technology provides a detailed record of responses for later analysis.

4. Unlike traditional focus groups where the aim is to capture responses at the group level, technology-assisted focus groups capture both individual and group data. Individuals may be assigned specific dials so that responses are linked to a specific name or ID number. (When individual records are not helpful, dials may be randomly distributed so that each respondent remains anonymous.) Focus group data linked to identifiers can be merged with existing data sets to create robust assessment information.

Summary

The old adage "you get what you measure" reminds us to measure the things that matter the most. While new technologies extend our options, they may also produce a new adage, reminding us that "how you measure affects what you get." The three technologies reviewed here—web-based surveys, scannable survey forms, and technology-assisted focus groups—are new tools ready to support higher education assessment efforts. As with all assessment, we need to test our methods, use multiple methods when possible, and never forget the value of common sense and professional judgment in assessing first-year programs.

Using the SWOT Analysis to Assess a First-Year Program

Brenda C. Moore

How do you assess or evaluate a first-year program? What are the best methods of assessment? How do we validate our program to administrators? How do we collect data from a course required of all first-year students and thus void of a control group? Should the assessment be summative or formative? Qualitative or quantitative?

Most of us who are responsible for a first-year program and/or course have probably struggled with these and numerous other questions related to the assessment process.

Thanks to the Policy Center, Gardner-Webb University became involved in the Consortium for North Carolina Private Universities and has begun to try some different forms of assessment. In Fall 2000, we had several assessment committees working simultaneously: a strategic planning committee, a task-force to evaluate the first-year through the consortium, and program reviews for several programs requested by our president. I was asked to lead a review for our first-year program using a SWOT Analysis. The following report focuses on the SWOT Analysis and how we used the process for evaluation purposes.

Definition of SWOT Analysis

The SWOT Analysis originated in the business and marketing fields but can be adapted to higher education. According to Pride and Ferrell (2000) the SWOT Analysis is

> an assessment of an organization's strengths, weaknesses, opportunities, and threats. Strengths refer to competitive advantages or core competencies that create an advantage in meeting the needs of its target markets. Weaknesses refer to limitations an organization might face in developing or implementing a marketing strategy. Opportunities refer to favorable conditions in the environment that could produce rewards for an organization if acted upon properly. Threats refer to conditions or barriers that may prevent the organization from reaching its objectives (p. 43).

Strengths and weaknesses are internal factors; opportunities and threats are external. It is easy to see how SWOT can be adapted to an educational program.

Since most SWOT Analyses are designed for "profit" organizations, and most universities are considered "non-profit," some of the terminology must be adjusted, but the concept itself fits. An article by Balamuralikrishna and Dugger (1995) reports that "management tools originally intended for industry can frequently be tailored for application in education due to fundamental similarities in the administrative duties of the respective chief executive officers." Perhaps assessment strategies are also similar enough to apply to both profit and non-profit organizations.

In our particular study, we found it helpful to look at the first-year program as a separate entity of the university. This perspective seemed the most effective way to make use of opportunities and threats as external factors in our assessment process. Pride and Ferrell (2000) suggest that the best way to differentiate between a weakness (internal) and a threat (external) is to ask the question, "Would this issue exist if the company did not exist? If the answer is yes, then the issue should be considered external" (p. 43). For example, "the lack of available instructors (due to overloads)" surfaced as a threat to our program. Though we are an integral part of the university, we had to separate ourselves from it in order to understand this as a true threat. The fact that the first-year program does not have its own faculty and must rely on the university faculty at large to staff the program is reason to consider this situation an external threat. The answer to Pride and Ferrell's question in this case is, "yes." If our first-year program did not exist, the university would still have faculty overload problems, which would ultimately affect other areas of the institution. We also asked ourselves the question, "Does this issue simply weaken the effectiveness of our program or does it actually threaten its very existence?" The answer, in our case, is clear. A lack of instructors is a major threat to our program; without teachers, we cannot offer the course. In this example, the threat is severe because the course is a core requirement for all incoming first-year students. SWOT helped us better understand this possible threat. Pride and Ferrell (2000) further point out that "threats must be acted upon to prevent them from limiting the capabilities of the organization" (p. 43). The lack of instructors (threat) forces us to take action or risk the consequences.

Procedures for Collecting and Reporting Data

In preparation for the SWOT Analysis, I decided to use e-mail to expedite communication and information gathering. Each of the University 101 instructors evaluated our program based on the SWOT format. I asked them to brainstorm and list their comments under the headings of strengths, weaknesses, opportunities, and threats. Their responses were organized in a chart. I included my comments on a separate chart, since my perspectives might vary from that of the other faculty. Our president specifically requested a brief report, so we used a four-column chart and entered short comments and phrases in each column. This provided a structured, concise format, allowed us to include a large amount of information in a small amount of space, and eliminated pages of narrative data. However, the SWOT could just as easily be summarized in an outline, a four-square matrix, a narrative, or a variety of other formats. The structure for organizing the information is flexible and should be determined based on who will be reviewing the data and how extensively the information will be used for further evaluation.

Examples of comments from our SWOT Analysis are provided below:

Strengths: assists students with adjustment and enhances college success; good support system for freshmen; inspires a sense of community; provides instant faculty advisor/mentor; quality of faculty; super training for teaching the course

Weaknesses: class sizes too large this year; only one hour of credit for two hours of class; advisee load excessive; too little contact [with academic advisor, also University 101 instructor] in spring semester for high-risk students

Opportunities: leadership development with implementation of peer mentor program; could be the best University 101 for private colleges anywhere; further improve retention; allows parents and students to meet University 101 instructors during orientation and see them as caring and approachable

Threats: lack of available faculty to teach; heavy advising loads; low administrative priority

These are just a few of the comments that surfaced from our faculty who teach the course. They are brief and to the point but give usable information about our program.

Pros and Cons of the SWOT Analysis

According to Pride and Ferrell, "the SWOT analysis framework has gained widespread acceptance because it is both a simple and powerful tool for marketing strategy development" (p. 44). Balamuralikrishna and Dugger (1995) add that it is "neither cumbersome nor time-consuming and is effective because of its simplicity." Simplicity and minimal time involvement make this a valuable evaluation tool for most organizations, particularly in the field of education and academia where constant assessment is required and needed but where time constraints make it a difficult task. As with other forms of qualitative research, the SWOT Analysis provides a rich data source, widely accessible to campus stakeholders without the necessity of detailed statistical analysis.

Drawbacks to SWOT Analysis do exist; Balamuralikrishna and Dugger (1995) note that SWOT analyses typically "reflect a person or group's perspectives and viewpoints on a situation which can be misused to justify a previously decided course of action rather than used as a means to open up new possibilities." Another disadvantage of SWOT may be that the same issue can be seen as both a threat and an opportunity, depending on the people or groups involved. A committee or institution must, therefore, remind itself that the purpose of the collected information is to evaluate the program effectively and honestly. Since the SWOT Analysis is a subjective type of evaluation, it may be important to consider that (a) the information collected is based on perceptions and interpretation, thus promoting varying insights into the situation, and (b) the information may be more vulnerable to manipulation by those seeking to satisfy their own interests. "New possibilities" may be viewed as threats by some, especially if they involve organizational change, budget increases, and/or additional resources. Balamuralikrishna and Dugger (1995) also emphasize that "SWOT offers a systematic approach of introspection into both positive and negative concerns." It is likely that this type of study will bring to the surface some negative concerns or perceptions, but these need not be a disadvantage to SWOT, if the purpose of the study is clear and the evaluation and decision-making process is fair.

One way to counteract misinterpretations of SWOT analyses is to gather information from a variety of persons or groups involved in the program under study, using alternate strategies. In our situation, we surveyed our first-year students to get their perspectives, thus confirming what faculty and administrators saw as strengths and weaknesses. We found that there were many similarities between faculty and student opinion. For example, SWOT analysis for faculty listed as a strength the mentor/advisor role and the "one-on-one" attention given to our first-year students. The course evaluation administered to students confirmed this as a strength by ranking it a 4.1 on a 5 point Likert scale. Since students are not privy to certain information, they could not confirm nor deny such issues as advising loads and low prioritization from administrators, which were two of our threats. But it is helpful to compare and see areas where we are on target.

Follow-Up

As with any evaluation tool, collecting and processing is counter-productive without follow-up. The ultimate goal, according to Berkowitz, Kerin, Hartley, and Rudelius (2000), is to identify the critical factors affecting the organization and then to build on vital strengths, correct (or minimize) glaring weaknesses, exploit (or seize) significant opportunities, and avoid (or counteract) disaster-laden threats.

Follow-up and attempts to effect change will be the task for us in the next couple of months. Our president may determine how and when we act on certain issues; but regardless of any directives from the administration, we know as director and faculty of the first-year program, that we have work to do.

Herein lies the challenge! It is crucial to turn the results of the analysis into specific actions. The ideal, of course, is to convert internal weaknesses into strengths and external threats into opportunities. For example, our situation would call for making a sufficient number of the best of our university faculty available to teach our first-year students so that retention would continue to improve, class sizes would decrease, and our program would reflect the "best" in our faculty by ultimately becoming the "best" in first-year programs. Such a response would play to our recognized threat of lack of available faculty while moving us toward an opportunity voiced by one of the current faculty members. Putting the results of a SWOT analysis into action can also be highly synergistic; when internal strengths are matched with external opportunities, the benefits are potentially endless!

Summary

The SWOT Analysis can be an excellent tool for assessing where an institution or program is, and exploring the possibilities of where it could be. It offers the opportunity to evaluate a program effectively and simply with input from involved individuals and provides concise statements that can be used for strategic planning. It further offers opportunities for an institution to develop collected information into goals and objectives. Used effectively and creatively, SWOT can help programs and universities improve and ultimately facilitate a higher level of excellence.

At Gardner-Webb University, the SWOT Analysis was particularly effective because it collected information from an array of constituencies, provided a guide for organizing data, was powerful in reporting and comparing the "voice" of students and faculty, was concise and easy to read, was balanced (i.e., not overly pessimistic or falsely optimistic), and provided information for action and improvement.

References

Balamuralikrishna, R., & Dugger, J. (1995) SWOT analysis: A management tool for initiating new programs in vocational schools. [Electronic version]. *Journal of Vocational and Technical Education, 12*(1).

Berkowitz, E. N., Kerin, R. A., Hartley, S. W., & Rudelius, W. (2000). *Marketing* (6th ed.). Boston: Irwin/McGraw Hill.

Pride, W. M., & Ferrell, O. C. (2000). *Marketing: Concepts and strategies 2000.* (Library ed.). Boston: Houghton Mifflin.

The Power of Benchmarking

Glenn Detrick &
Joseph A. Pica

Since the inception of the total quality management (TQM) movement, the power of comparative assessment has been well documented in the private sector. Benchmarking is broadly defined as a comparison of similar processes across public and/or private organizations to identify best practices in an effort to improve organizational performance. When conducting benchmarking studies, investigators typically measure performance, systematically identify best practices, learn from leading organizations, and recommend best practices for adoption as appropriate to the organization. Short, medium, and long-range action plans are typically created as a result of these studies. However, benchmarking has only recently been effectively introduced to higher education settings. With the introduction of high quality national benchmarking studies, institutions in higher education have finally begun to recognize the value of benchmarking as an assessment methodology to support introspection, strategic planning, and continuous improvement initiatives. One example of this approach is a recent partnership between Educational Benchmarking, Inc. (EBI) and the Policy Center on the First Year of College. Using data collected by EBI, the Policy Center has undertaken a benchmarking study to compare the efficacy and effectiveness of first-year seminars.

While there are many approaches to benchmarking, we will focus our attention here on studies that assess stakeholder perceptions of quality. The principles of stakeholder benchmarking studies are well suited to assist colleges and universities in the development of a comprehensive, long-term assessment strategy. Stakeholder benchmarking is effective because it addresses two aspects essential to the continuous quality improvement process: (a) identifying the factors most important for improving quality and (b) initiating and sustaining the process of change essential for continuous quality improvement. The Policy Center/EBI study is focusing on students enrolled in first-year seminars as the key stakeholder.

Why Benchmarking Is a Powerful Continuous Quality Improvement Tool

It Assesses What is Most Important

Successful benchmarking assessment studies evaluate the degree to which an organization is successfully fulfilling its mission from the perspective of key stakeholders. If you believe in the old adage "you get what you measure," it is essential that assessment studies focus on mission-critical factors. A successful and high-quality benchmarking study will identify and assess the factors critical to the successful fulfillment of the mission. Experts in the mission of a particular discipline ensure that instruments capture the factors essential to that mission and determine the content of the studies.

It Challenges Long-Held Beliefs

Benchmarking studies provide a comprehensive internal and comparative evaluation of performance serving to identify strengths and weaknesses. Educators (and others as well) have a tendency to overestimate their strengths and underestimate their weaknesses (evidenced by the 50 or so schools who contend to be in the "top 20" of any ranking). Little progress can be made when performance evaluation is left to a debate based solely on experience and anecdotal evidence.

Benchmarking studies can provide comprehensive, credible results to guide and motivate those in a position to have the greatest impact on quality improvement. When professionals review benchmarking results, inevitably two types of conclusions are reached. First, a good percentage of the results reinforce what professionals already believe, based on their previous education, training, and experience in the field. This falls under the category of "we knew this all along." This is to be expected from professionals who have years of experience. The difference is that now there is credible, comprehensive, comparable evidence to support what was previously opinion or supposition.

Second, professionals are inevitably presented with evidence that is contrary to long-held assumptions and typically question the results for this reason. Once the credibility of the results has been established, professionals face the challenge of integrating the new information into their overall view of performance. These results typically have the greatest impact on the improvement process. Credible results provide evidence for professionals to rethink their assumptions about strengths and weaknesses. It requires them to incorporate new insights into a revised perspective of problems and opportunities. Benchmarking results raise questions about previously held beliefs and challenge professionals to address the issues most critical to improved efficiency and effectiveness.

Benchmarking Informs Decision Making

Few organizations have unlimited resources to invest in all aspects of their operation. Each year educators are faced with making resource allocation decisions that will result in the accomplishment of their mission. One of the major barriers to change is the inability of managers to shift resources from historically established budget lines. Stakeholder benchmarking studies can provide information that details the level of performance as well as the importance of factors to stakeholders' perceptions of quality. Identifying low performance factors that have great impact on perceived quality allows managers to focus their attention and deploy their resources in the most efficient and effective manner. It prioritizes for the decision-maker where an investment of resources will have the greatest impact on improving performance in the eyes of key stakeholders.

It is essential to understand both areas of strength and weakness and the importance of the factors to overall satisfaction of stakeholders. For example, the factor with the lowest performance score may not be the factor that is most important to constituents' overall satisfaction. By identifying the factors that are predictors of overall satisfaction in order of importance, educators are able to identify exactly where their resources will have the most positive impact on performance. Simply stated, it is possible for benchmarking studies to identify where managers should invest their resources to have the greatest positive impact on performance. Solid evidence of performance and identifying which factors are important for improving quality provide managers with the information they need to shift resources.

Benchmarking Motivates Staff

Even the most well-intentioned faculty and administrators become frustrated and discouraged when they receive little feedback regarding the impact of their efforts. Benchmarking motivates staff members in four ways:

1. It reinforces performance. Evidence of good performance is an opportunity to congratulate and reward staff members for a job well done, serving to reinforce and motivate them to maintain and improve performance.
2. It identifies mission-critical factors essential for quality improvement and provides the staff with evidence of where their efforts will have the greatest positive impact on improving performance. Benchmarking results identify for staff members the areas most important for improving overall performance on mission-critical factors. Identifying areas where the performance is below that of peers/competitors has the effect of challenging the staff to improve performance by tapping into their competitive nature.
3. It provides meaningful performance comparisons. Comparative results with selected peers remove all doubt that it "can't be done by anyone else better than we are doing it." With evidence that others perform at a higher level, staff typically rise to the challenge and commit themselves to improvement.
4. It provides continuous assessment. With a continuous benchmarking process, staff members come to know what needs to be improved and recognize how and when their performance will be assessed in the future. Knowing performance will be measured and evaluated over time has proven to be a powerful motivator.

The Essential Characteristics of Successful Benchmarking

Benchmarking takes many forms and has been associated with many processes. From our experience, the following are essential to successful benchmarking studies. Such studies must be:

Credible

Studies must be designed to gather feedback on aspects of the program that are directly related to the successful fulfillment of the organization's mission. Examples of performance measures that are critical to success include stakeholders' perceptions and resource allocations. Most importantly, respected professionals from the field must be involved in the development of the content of the study. The statistical reliability and validity should far exceed the minimum standards recognized by academics for statistically sound studies.   Studies conducted by thoughtful external organizations increase credibility.

Comparative

National survey instruments ensure comparability of results across the profession. Comparison with a small set of peers selected by participating institutions is essential for providing valid benchmarks for performance. Comparisons that only provide national standards or comparisons with predetermined groups do not provide the benchmarks necessary to evaluate performance most accurately. Studies must either include only schools who see themselves as peers or they must allow each participating school to select the schools to be included in their results analysis to assure comparisons are relevant.

Confidential

There are two levels of confidentiality: one to protect the identity of the individual participants and the other to assure that results are not used to the disadvantage of any participating institution. Based on the scope and breadth of the study, each benchmarking group must determine the importance of confidentiality. The criteria for establishing levels of confidentially are based on the legality of sharing the information, the trust among the participants, the sensitivity of the data, and the ultimate use of the data once the results are distributed to participating institutions. One of the most important issues is whether the results can be publicly released, allowing the participants to indicate their performance is better than their peers/competitors, individually or as a group.   For example, EBI benchmarking studies are for internal, continuous improvement purposes only and results may not be used for marketing purposes.

Comprehensive

The data from benchmarking studies should be analyzed to provide summaries that identify areas of strength and weakness in a variety of ways. Descriptive and prescriptive statistical analyses should be provided to identify statistical differences between means and factors that are most critical to overall satisfaction. The results should be designed to provide decision-makers with information they need to deploy resources more effectively and alter processes directly related to quality improvement.

Continuous

Individual institutional results should be analyzed longitudinally to provide a comprehensive picture of the success of change initiatives and overall progress over time. Longitudinal analysis allows institutions to evaluate changes each year that result in improvements in performance. Longitudinal analysis provides the feedback to evaluate continually initiatives implemented to improve quality. This iterative cycle of initiating changes and evaluating performance results is central to the continuous quality improvement process.

The Relationship Between Continuous Participation and Continuous Improvement

In three recent EBI studies, two in management education and one in residence halls, schools that participated annually for at least three years realized statistically significant improvement on 96% of the factors. While the correlation does not allow us to make causal inferences, it does raise interesting questions about the relationship between continuous participation in benchmarking assessment studies and continuous improvement.

Summary

The power of benchmarking to serve as a catalyst for continuous improvement rests with no single element but rather with the synergistic integration of a range of elements. Benchmarking studies that are credible, comparative, comprehensive, confidential, and continuous have the greatest potential for supporting change initiatives. The success of a continuous improvement benchmarking strategy is based on educating management and staff regarding the benchmarking principles and practices. At their heart, benchmarking studies both reinforce and challenge assumptions. Continuous improvement is rooted in an individual's ability to accept information contrary to long held beliefs and use the information to reinterpret their strategy for initiating and sustaining improvement.

Tools For Assessing the First-Year Student Experience

George D. Kuh

Among the more important things an institution should know about the first-year experience are what new students think they will do in college and what they actually do. The short version of this argument goes like this.

What students do in college and how they use an institution's resources for learning are critical to their success broadly defined, including academic achievement, satisfaction, and persistence. Students do better academically and socially when they apportion reasonable chunks of time to a combination of the right kinds of activities—such educationally purposeful things as studying; interacting with faculty members, advisors, and right-minded peers; performing community service; and participating in cocurricular activities. For colleges and universities to induce such desirable behavior from more of their students on a more frequent basis they need to first determine how students are spending their time during the critical first year of college and to what extent students' expectations for the first year are consistent with the institution's and the students' own aspirations. All the better if benchmarks are available from comparable institutions because this kind of information is especially powerful in getting faculty members and administrators to focus their attention on areas that can make a demonstrable difference in increasing the quality of the first-year experience.

Fortunately, some reliable assessment tools for obtaining such information are readily available to educators.

Elsewhere in this collection, Peter Ewell and Karl Schilling note the importance of expectations to a successful first-year experience. One of the Seven Principles for Good Practice in Undergraduate Education is to communicate high expectations. As Chickering and Gamson (1987) urge, "Expect more and you will get more" (p. 5). To maximize learning and involvement during the first year of college, students need to set personal learning goals. These goals should be challenging enough so that they must try their best in classes and make use of campus resources to augment classroom learning and to help them attain their learning goals. Discovering what students expect of and from their college experience is crucial if faculty are to adjust their instructional approaches accordingly and institutions are to modify policies and practices to respond in educationally effective ways to the current generation of college students.

We developed the College Student Expectations Questionnaire (CSXQ) for use in a FIPSE-funded project that Karl and Karen Maitland Schilling directed several years ago. The CSXQ (Kuh & Pace, 1998) is a shortened version of its parent instrument, the College Student Experiences Questionnaire (CSEQ) which was developed by Bob Pace (1990). Both surveys provide information about the substance and quality of effort students put forth in various activities that contribute to their learning and personal development, such as interacting with faculty and peers, reading and writing, using the library and other campus facilities, and taking advantage of cultural events. In the case of the CSXQ, students are asked just prior to the start of classes (such as during summer orientation or fall welcome week) to estimate what they expect to do during their first year of college. Curriculum committees, student affairs staff, and others can then examine these data in order to gauge whether student expectations are realistic in terms of the institution's mission and learning goals. The information can also be used to modify new student recruitment materials and orientation activities if it is discovered that student expectations need to be modified in order for students to succeed.

Indiana University, Miami University, and some other schools have administered the CSEQ (Pace & Kuh, 1998) near the end of the spring semester to first-year students who completed the CSXQ the previous fall to determine the degree to which students realized their own expectations for taking advantage of learning opportunities. These projects typically show that in most areas students have greater expectations for their first year than they subsequently achieve. That is, they study fewer hours, write less, and interact with faculty members less than they expect to and less than faculty would like. This pattern of results prompts questions about whether the nature and amount of assigned academic work is appropriate to cultivate the range and depth of intellectual skills required to succeed in college and beyond. At my campus, students' background characteristics were less important to their post-matriculation engagement, achievement, and persistence than what they expected from college. Indeed, expecting to engage in the intellectual and cultural life of the campus was the most powerful predictor of subsequently engaging in the broader academic and social dimensions of college life typically associated with a rich undergraduate experience (Olsen, Kuh, Schilling, Schilling, Connolly, Simmons, & Vesper, 1998). To get more information about the CSEQ and CSXQ, visit the CSEQ web site hosted by Indiana University.

Among the other tools available to assess what students do in the first year of college is The College Student Report (Kuh, 2000), the survey instrument developed for the National Survey of Student Engagement (NSSE). The NSSE is a national study funded by The Pew Charitable Trusts and co-sponsored by The Carnegie Foundation for the Advancement of Teaching and The Pew Forum on Undergraduate Learning. The Report is conceptually similar to the CSEQ in that it measures student engagement in good educational practices and also contains some new items. The first two years of the NSSE gathered results from about 88,000 first-year and senior students from about 470 different four-year colleges and universities. The large number of schools allows us to establish benchmarks for different types of institutions and students. The NSSE can also be a source of longitudinal information about the college student experience by surveying first-year respondents again when they are seniors (Kuh, 2001). More information about the NSSE project, including registration information for future surveys, is available on the NSSE web site hosted by Indiana University.

Having a lot of good information about the first year will not make any difference if it just sits on a shelf. As Trudy Banta and I have argued elsewhere (Banta & Kuh, 1998; Kuh & Banta, 2000), a cross-functional, campus-level assessment committee made up of faculty members, academic and student affairs administrators, students, and others must be involved in selecting what kind of data the institution needs, carefully considering what the data mean, and then deciding what interventions are warranted to improve the first-year experience and to increase the institution's effectiveness. Ignorance is no longer an excuse, given that some decent assessment tools are already available and that there are more on the way, thanks in part to the Pew-funded Policy Center on the First Year of College and related initiatives.

References

Banta, T. W., & Kuh, G. D. (1998). A missing link in assessment: Collaboration between academic and student affairs. *Change, 30*(2), 40-46.

Chickering, A. W., & Gamson, Z. F. (1987). Seven principles for good practice in undergraduate education. *AAHE Bulletin, 39*(7), 3-7.

Kuh, G. D. (2000). The College Student Report. National Survey of Student Engagement, Center for Postsecondary Research and Planning. Bloomington: Indiana University.

Kuh, G. D. (2001). Assessing what really matters to student learning: Inside the National Survey of Student Engagement. *Change, 33*(3), 10-17, 66.

Kuh, G. D., & Banta, T. W. (2000). Faculty-student affairs collaboration on assessment: Lessons from the field. *About Campus, 4*(6), 4-11.

Kuh, G. D., & Pace, C. R. (1998). College Student Expectations Questionnaire (2nd ed.). Center for Postsecondary Research and Planning. Bloomington: Indiana University.

Olsen, D. Kuh, G. D., Schilling, K. M., Schilling, K., Connolly, M. R., Simmons, A., & Vesper, N. (1998, November). *Great expectations: What first-year students say they will do and what they actually do.* Paper presented at the annual meeting of the Association for the Study of Higher Education, Miami.

Pace, C. R. (1990). *College Student Experiences Questionnaire.* (3rd ed.). Los Angeles: University of California, Los Angeles, Center for the Study of Evaluation (Available from the Center for Postsecondary Research and Planning, Indiana University).

Pace, C. R., & Kuh, G. D. (1998). *College Student Experience Questionnaire.* (4th ed.). Center for Postsecondary Research and Planning. Bloomington: Indiana University.

Course-Evaluation Surveys and the First-Year Seminar: Recommendations for Use[1]

Joseph B. Cuseo

The quality of teaching that first-year students experience in introductory courses may shape their overall attitude toward the college experience and establish an anticipatory "set" influencing their approach to learning throughout their subsequent years in college. As Kenneth Spear argues in *Rejuvenating Introductory Courses* (1984), "In these formative experiences, [first-year students] learn what it is to be a student, what is required to get by, what it means to acquire an education" (p. 6). Recognizing the shaping potential of college teaching, Erickson and Strommer (1991) argue that the instruction of first-year students should be made an institutional priority.

Student course-evaluation surveys (student ratings) continue to be the most commonly employed method for assessing the effectiveness of first-year teaching in general and the impact of first-year seminars in particular. National research reveals that student ratings are the most widely used source of information for assessing teaching effectiveness in college (Seldin, 1993), and student ratings of the course or course instructor are the most commonly used strategy for assessing the new-student seminars (Barefoot & Fidler, 1996). But do these evaluations provide an accurate picture of what happens in the college classroom? Should we take them seriously?

The discussion that follows provides information and recommendations concerning student course evaluations and is organized around the following issues:

1. Why we should take student evaluations seriously
2. How to construct a valid course-evaluation instrument
3. How to administer course evaluations in a fashion that increases their reliability and validity
4. How to analyze, summarize, and report the results of course evaluations in a manner that serves to increase their interpretability, potential for instructional improvement, and capacity for demonstrating causal impact on student outcomes

---

[1] *Editor's Note:* This is a condensed version of Cuseo's original remarks on assessment. The text of the entire piece can be accessed on the web site of The Policy Center on the First Year of College.

The Case for Student Evaluation of College Courses

One major strength of student evaluations is that their reliability and validity have probably received more empirical support than any other method of instructional assessment—there have been over 1,300 articles and books published which contain research on the topic of student ratings (Cashin, 1988). There are perennial criticisms of student evaluations by some faculty and some isolated studies purportedly refute their validity, yet when the results of all studies are viewed collectively and synthesized, they provide strong support for the following conclusions.

♦ Students' judgments correlate positively (i.e., are in agreement with) the judgments of more experienced observers (e.g., alumni, teaching assistants, faculty peers, administrators, and trained external observers (Aleamoni & Hexner, 1980; Feldman, 1988, 1989; Marsh, 1984).

♦ Students can evaluate what is taught and how it is taught, and these evaluations are not unduly influenced by their own personal characteristics—such as gender or academic ability, or by characteristics extraneous to the course—such as time of day or time of year when the course is taught (Abrami, Perry, & Leventhal, 1982; Aleamoni & Hexner, 1980; Feldman, 1977; 1979; Seldin, 1993).

♦ Students' overall ratings of course quality and teaching effectiveness correlate positively with what they actually learn in the course—as measured by their performance on standardized final exams. In other words, students rate most highly those courses in which they learn the most and those instructors from whom they learn the most (Abrami, d'Apollonia, & Rosenfield, 1997; Centra, 1977; Cohen, 1981, 1986; McCallum, 1984).

♦ Student evaluations do not depend heavily on the student's age (Centra, 1993) or level of college experience. For example, lower-division students (first-year students and sophomores) do not provide ratings that differ systematically from upper-division students (juniors and seniors) (McKeachie, 1979).

♦ Students distinguish or discriminate among specific dimensions and components of course instruction. For example, students give independent ratings to such course dimensions as course organization, instructor-student rapport, and the quality of course assignments (Marsh, 1984). As Aleamoni (1987) illustrates, "If a teacher tells great jokes, he or she will receive high ratings in humor . . . but these ratings do not influence students' assessments of other teaching skills" (p. 27).

Moreover, a large body of research has consistently refuted commonly held myths about student ratings. For instance, the following findings fail to support traditional criticisms of student evaluations.

♦ Students who receive higher course grades do not give higher course ratings (Theall, Franklin, & Ludlow, 1990; Howard & Maxwell, 1980, 1982).

♦ Students do not give lower ratings to difficult or challenging courses that require a heavy workload (Marsh & Dunkin, 1992; Sixbury & Cashin, 1995).

♦ The instructor's personality and popularity do not unduly influence student evaluations; for example, entertaining teachers do not necessarily receive higher overall student ratings (Costin, Greenough, & Menges, 1971; McKeachie, Lin, Moffett, & Daugherty, 1978; Marsh & Ware, 1982).

♦ Student ratings do not change over time or with students' post-course experiences; in contrast, there is substantial agreement between student evaluations given at the time of course completion and retrospective evaluations given by the same students one-to-five years later (Feldman, 1989; Overall & Marsh, 1980). This refutes the oft-cited argument that students are immature and only with maturity, or the passage of time, will they come to appreciate courses or instructors that were initially rated poorly.

Course-evaluation surveys or questionnaires are also capable of generating an extensive amount of data on a large sample of respondents in a relatively short period of time. If a student-rating survey or questionnaire is well constructed and carefully administered, it can be an effective and efficient vehicle for assessing the attitudes, perspectives, and self-reported outcomes of the institution's most valued constituent: its learners.

The degree of reliability and validity of a particular student-rating survey can be influenced by the content (items) of the survey and the process by which it is administered. The next two sections offer strategies for maximizing the validity, interpretability, and usefulness of student course evaluations. Many of these recommendations are also relevant for improving the effectiveness of surveys designed to solicit faculty/staff evaluations of instructor training programs offered in conjunction with a new-student seminar.

Recommendations Regarding the Construction of the Course-Evaluation Instrument

1. *Cluster individual items into logical categories that represent important course objectives or instructional components.* The items that compose the course-evaluation instrument could be the stated objectives of the course, and similar objectives could be clustered into separate sections. Items could also be grouped together in separate sections relating to the following key components of college instruction (a) course planning and design (e.g., questions pertaining to overall course organization and clarity of course objectives); (b) classroom instruction (e.g., items pertaining to in-class teaching, such as clarity and organization of lectures or instructional presentations); (c) evaluation of student performance (e.g., items pertaining to the fairness of tests, assignments, grading practices, and the quality of feedback provided by the instructor). Also, a healthy balance of questions pertaining to both course *content* (e.g., topics and subtopics) and instructional *process* (e.g., in-class and out-of-class learning activities) should be included on the evaluation form. For a discussion of the advantages of these strategies, see Cuseo's (1999) discussion of evaluating instructor training programs.

2. *Provide a rating scale that allows five-to-seven choice points or response options.* Research evidence suggests that fewer than five choices reduces the instrument's ability to discriminate between satisfied and dissatisfied respondents, and more than seven options adds nothing to the instrument's discriminability (Cashin, 1990).

3. *If possible, do not include the neutral "don't know" or "not sure" as a response option.* This alternative could generate misleading results because it may be used as an "escape route" by students who do have strong opinions but are reluctant to offer them (Arreola, 1983).

4. *Include items that ask students to report their behavior.* Astin's (1991) taxonomy for classifying types of assessment data includes two broad categories: (a)

psychological data reflecting students' internal states and (b) behavioral data reflecting students' activities. Traditionally, student course evaluations have focused almost exclusively on the gathering of psychological data (student perceptions or opinions). However, given that one of the major goals of most new-student seminars is to increase students' actual use of campus services and student involvement in campus life (Barefoot & Fidler, 1996), items which generate behavioral data pertaining to the use of campus services, or frequency of participation in cocurricular activities, should also be included on the evaluation instrument.

5. *Beneath each question or item to be rated, print the word "comments" and leave a small space for any written remarks students would like to make with respect to that particular item.* Written comments often serve to clarify or elucidate numerical ratings, and instructors frequently report that written comments are most useful for course-improvement purposes, especially if such comments are specific (Seldin, 1992).

Allowing students to write comments with respect to each individual item, rather than restricting them to a "general comments" section at the very end of the evaluation form, may serve to increase the specificity of students' written remarks and, consequently, their usefulness for course or program improvement.

6. *Include at least two global items on the evaluation instrument pertaining to overall course effectiveness or course impact; these items can be used for summative evaluation purposes.* The following statements illustrate global items that are useful for summative evaluation:

I would rate the overall quality of this course as (poor to excellent).
Comments:

I would rate the general usefulness of this course as (very low to very high).
Comments:

I would recommend this course to other first-year students: (strongly agree to strongly disagree).
Comments:

Responses to these global items can provide an effective and convenient summary or "summative" snapshot of students' overall evaluation of the course that can be readily used in program assessment reports. Research has repeatedly shown that these global ratings are more predictive of student learning than student ratings given to individual survey items pertaining to specific aspects or dimensions of course instruction (Braskamp & Ory, 1994; Centra, 1993; Cohen, 1986). As Cashin (1990) puts it, global items function "like a final course grade" (p. 2). For additional discussion of the use of global items in survey development, see Cuseo's (1999) discussion of evaluating instructor training programs.

7. *Include an open-ended question asking for written comments about the course's strengths and weaknesses, and ask how the latter may be rectified.* Such questions can often provide useful information about students' general reaction to the course as well as specific suggestions for course improvement. For example, in a new-student seminar, students could be asked to provide a written response to a question that asks them to "describe a major change (if any) in their approach to the college experience that resulted from their participation in the course." Or, students could be asked, "Was there anything important to learn about being a successful student that was not addressed in the course?" The written responses to these questions

provided by students in separate class sections could be aggregated and their content analyzed to identify recurrent themes or response categories.

8. *Provide some space at the end of the evaluation form so that individual instructors can add their own questions* (Seldin, 1993). This practice enables instructors to assess specific instructional practices that are unique to their courses. Also, this option should serve to give instructors some sense of personal control or ownership of the evaluation instrument that, in turn, may increase their motivation to use the results in a constructive fashion.

9. *Give students the opportunity to suggest questions they think should be included on the evaluation form.* This opportunity could be cued by a prompt at the end of the evaluation form, such as, "Suggested Questions for Future Evaluations." This practice has three major advantages: (a) It may identify student perspectives and concerns that the evaluation form failed to address, (b) it shows respect for student input, and (c) it gives students some sense of control or ownership of the evaluation process.

10. *Complete a pilot study of the evaluation.* To improve the reliability and validity of campus-specific instruments that are designed internally, a pilot study of the instrument should be conducted on a small sample of students to assess whether the instrument's instructions are clear, the wording of each of its items is unambiguous, and the total time needed to complete the instrument is manageable.

Recommendations Regarding the Wording (Phrasing) of Individual Items

When soliciting information on the incidence or frequency of an experienced event (e.g., "How often have you seen your advisor this semester?"), avoid response options that require high levels of inference on the part of the reader (e.g., "rarely," "occasionally," "frequently"). Instead, provide options in the form of numbers or frequency counts that require less inference or interpretation by the reader (e.g., 0, 1–2, 3–4, 5 or more times). This practice should serve to reduce the likelihood that individual students will interpret the meaning of response options in different ways.

When asking students to rate their degree of involvement or satisfaction with a campus support service or student activity, be sure to include a zero or "not used" option. This response alternative allows a valid choice for those students who may have never experienced the service or activity in question (Astin, 1991).

For additional recommendations on the wording of survey items, see Cuseo's (1999) discussion of evaluating instructor training programs.

Recommendations for Administration of Course Evaluations

The amount of time allotted for students to complete their evaluations should be standardized across different sections of the same course. Another temporal factor for consideration is the time during the academic term or semester when course evaluations should be administered. One option is to administer the evaluations immediately after the final exam of the course. This provides two advantages. First, it allows students to assess the whole course because the final exam represents its last key component. Second, students are not likely to be absent on the day of the final exam, so a larger and more representative sample of students would be present to complete the course evaluation than if it were administered on a regular class day. Perhaps the best approach is for course instructors to agree to administer the evaluation instrument as close to the end of the course as possible (e.g., during the last week of the term), but not immediately after the final exam. This approach would also better accommodate those instructors who elect not to administer a final examination in the course.

Instructions read to students immediately before distribution of the evaluation forms should be standardized for all course instructors and all course sections. Some research has shown that student ratings can be affected by the wording of instructions that are read to students just prior to administration of the evaluation instrument (Pasen, Frey, Menges, & Rath, 1978). For instance, students tend to provide more favorable or lenient ratings if the instructions indicate that the evaluation results will be used for decisions about the instructor's "retention and promotion," as opposed to students being told that the results will be used for the purpose of "course improvement" or "instructional improvement" (Braskamp & Ory, 1994; Feldman, 1979).

Thus, instructions read to students in different sections of the course should be consistent (e.g., the same set of typewritten instructions read in each class).

To increase student motivation for course evaluation and to improve the validity of the results obtained, instructions read to students prior to course evaluation should include an explanation of why the evaluation is being conducted, a reminder that the evaluation is an opportunity for students to provide feedback that may improve the quality of the course for future generations, and an assurance that their evaluations will be taken seriously by both the program director and the course instructor. Students should also be encouraged to provide written comments and be reminded that specific comments often provide instructors with the best information on how to improve the course.

The behavior of instructors during the time when students complete their evaluations should be standardized. The importance of this practice is supported by research indicating that student ratings tend to be higher when the instructor remains in the room while students complete the course-evaluation form (Centra, 1993; Feldman, 1989; Marsh & Dunkin, 1992). The simplest and most direct way to eliminate this potential bias is for the instructor to be out of the room while students complete their evaluations (Seldin, 1993). This would require someone other than the instructor to administer the evaluations, such as a student government representative or a staff member. Whatever the procedure used, the bottom line is that variations in how instructors behave while students complete course evaluations should be minimized so that they do not unduly influence or "contaminate" the validity of student evaluations of the course.

Recommendations for Analyzing, Summarizing, and Reporting the Results of Course Evaluations

Report both the central tendency and variability of students' course ratings. Two key descriptive statistics can effectively summarize student ratings: (a) Mean (average) rating per item, which summarizes the central tendency of student ratings and (b) standard deviation (SD) per item, which summarizes the variation or spread of student ratings for each item.

In addition to computing the means and standard deviations for student ratings received by individual instructors in their own course sections, these statistics can also be computed for all class sections combined, thereby allowing individual instructors to compare the mean and standard deviation score for ratings in their own section with the composite mean and standard deviation calculated for all sections. Computing section-specific and across-section (composite) means and standard deviations for each item on the evaluation instrument also allows for the application of statistical tests to detect significant differences between the instructor's section-specific ratings and the average rating of all course sections combined. The results of these significance tests could provide valuable information that can be used for instructional diagnosis and improvement.

The identification and sharing of strategies for instructional improvement should be an essential component of course assessment, and it is a form of feedback that has been commonly ignored or overlooked when student ratings are used to evaluate college courses (Stevens, 1987; Cohen, 1990). One non-threatening way to provide course instructors with specific strategies for instructional improvement is to create opportunities for instructors to share concrete teaching practices that have worked for them. Strategies could be solicited specifically for each item on the evaluation form and a compendium of item-specific strategies could then be sent to all instructors—ideally, at the same time they receive the results of their course evaluations. In this fashion, instructors are not only provided with a descriptive summary of student-evaluation results, but also with a prescriptive summary of specific strategies about what they can do to improve their instructional performance with respect to each item on the evaluation instrument.

Comparing evaluations of the first-year seminar with those of other first-year courses can provide a reference point for interpreting student perceptions of the first-year seminar. To ensure a fair basis of comparison and a valid reference point, compare student evaluations of the course with other courses of similar class size (e.g., a first-year course in English composition) because there is some evidence that class size can influence student ratings, with smaller classes tending to receive slightly higher average ratings than larger classes (Cashin, 1988; Feldman, 1984). Moreover, first-semester courses that have the same required or elective status are likely to produce less variance in responses than those of different statuses.

Summary

Given that first-year initiatives continue to occupy peripheral status at many institutions (Barefoot, 2000), it becomes imperative that any effort to improve the quality of education for first-year students must be rigorously assessed to combat critics and silence skeptics. While such rigorous assessment may contribute to the improvement of first-year courses, it also has the potential to serve as a model for encouraging more careful assessment of all general education courses that form the foundation of the college curriculum.

References

Abrami, P. C., d'Apollonia, S., & Rosenfield, S. (1997). The dimensionality of student ratings of instruction: What we know and what we do not. In J. Smart (Ed.), *Higher education: Handbook of theory and research, Vol. II.* New York: Agathon Press.

Abrami, P. C., Perry, R. P., & Leventhal, L. (1982). The relationship between student personality characteristics, teacher ratings, and student achievement. *Journal of Educational Psychology, 74*(1), 111-125.

Aleamoni, L. M. (1987). Techniques for evaluating and improving instruction. *New Directions for Teaching and Learning, 31.* San Francisco: Jossey-Bass.

Aleamoni, L. M. & Hexner, P. Z. (1980). A review of the research on student evaluation and a report on the effect of different sets of instructions on student course and instructor evaluation. *Instructional Science, 9*(1), 67-84.

Arreola, R. A. (1983). Establishing successful faculty evaluation and development programs. In A. Smith (Ed.), Evaluating faculty and staff. *New Directions for Community Colleges, 41.* San Francisco: Jossey-Bass.

Astin, A. W. (1991). *Assessment for excellence: The philosophy and practice of assessment and evaluation in higher education.* New York: Macmillan.

Barefoot, B. O. (2000). The first-year experience—Are we making it any better? *About Campus, 4*(6), 12-18.

Barefoot, B. O., & Fidler, P. P. (1996). *The 1994 survey of freshman seminar programs: Continuing innovations in the collegiate curriculum.* (Monograph No. 20). Columbia, SC: University of South Carolina, National Resource Center for The Freshman Year Experience & Students in Transition.

Braskamp, L. A., & Ory, J. C. (1994). *Assessing faculty work: Enhancing individual and institutional performance.* San Francisco: Jossey-Bass.

Cashin, W. E. (1988). Student ratings of teaching: A summary of the research. *IDEA Paper No. 20.* Manhattan, Kansas: Kansas State University, Center for Faculty Evaluation and Development. (ERIC Document Reproduction No. ED 302 567)

Cashin, W. E. (1990). Students do rate different academic fields differently. In M. Theall, & J. Franklin (Eds.), Student ratings of instruction: Issues for improving practice (pp. 113-121). *New Directions for Teaching and Learning, 43.* San Francisco: Jossey Bass.

Centra, J. A. (1977). Student ratings of instruction and their relationship to student learning. *American Educational Research Journal, 14*(1), 17-24.

Centra, J. A. (1993). *Reflective faculty evaluation: Enhancing teaching and determining faculty effectiveness.* San Francisco: Jossey-Bass.

Cohen, P. A. (1981). Student ratings of instruction and student achievement: A Meta-analysis of multi-section validity studies. *Review of Educational Research, 51*(3), 281-309.

Cohen, P. A. (1986). *An updated and expanded meta-analysis of multi-section student rating validity studies.* Paper presented at the annual meeting of the American Educational Research Association, San Francisco, 1986.

Cohen, P. A. (1990). Bringing research into practice. In M. Theall & J. Franklin (Eds.), Student ratings of instruction: Issues for improving practice. *New Directions for Teaching and Learning, 43.* San Francisco: Jossey-Bass.

Costin, F., Greenough, W., & Menges, R. (1971). Student rated college teaching: Reliability, validity, and usefulness. *Review of Educational Research, 41*(5), 511-535.

Cuseo, J. B. (1999). Assessment and evaluation of instructor training programs. In M. S. Hunter & T. L. Skipper (Eds.), *Solid foundations: Building success for first-year seminars through instructor training and development* (Monograph No. 29) (pp. 91-105). Columbia, SC: University of South Carolina, National Resource Center for The First-Year Experience and Students in Transition.

Dressel, P. L. (1976). *Handbook of academic evaluation.* San Francisco: Jossey-Bass.

Erickson, B. L., & Strommer, D. W. (1991). *Teaching college freshmen.* San Francisco: Jossey-Bass.

Feldman, K. A. (1977). Consistency and variability among college students in rating their teachers and courses: A review and analysis. *Research in Higher Education, 6*(3), 233-274.

Feldman, K. A. (1979). The significance of circumstances for college students' ratings of their teachers and courses. *Research in Higher Education, 10*(2), 149-172.

Feldman, K. A. (1984). Class size and college students' evaluations of teachers and courses: A closer look. *Research in Higher Education, 21*(1), 45-116.

Feldman, K. A. (1988). Effective college teaching from the students' and faculty's view: Matched or mismatched priorities? *Research in Higher Education, 28*(4), 291-344.

Feldman, K. A. (1989). Instructional effectiveness of college teachers as judged by teachers themselves, current and former students, colleagues, administrators, and external (neutral) observers. *Research in Higher Education, 30*(2), 137-194.

Howard, G. S., & Maxwell, S. E. (1980). Correlation between student satisfaction and grades: A case of mistaken causation. *Journal of Educational Psychology, 72*(6), 810-820.

Howard, G. S., & Maxwell, S. E. (1982). Do grades contaminate student evaluations of instruction? *Research in Higher Education, 16*, 175-188.

Marsh, H. W. (1984). Students' evaluations of university teaching: Dimensionality, reliability, validity, potential biases, and utility. *Journal of Educational Psychology, 76*(5), 707-754.

Marsh, H. W., & Dunkin, M. (1992). Students' evaluations of university teaching: A multidimensional perspective. In J. C. Smart (Ed.*)*, *Higher education: Handbook of theory and research, Vol. 8* (pp. 143-233). New York: Agathon.

Marsh, H. W., & Ware, J. E., Jr. (1982). Effects of expressiveness, content coverage and incentive on multidimensional student rating scales: New interpretations of the Dr. Fox effect. *Journal of Educational Psychology, 74*(1), 126-134.

McCallum, L. W. (1984). A meta-analysis of course evaluation data and its use in the tenure decision. *Research in Higher Education, 21*(2), 150-158.

McKeachie, W. J. (1979). Student ratings of faculty: A reprise. *Academe, 65*(6), 384-397.

McKeachie, W. J., Lin, Y-G, Moffett, M., & Daugherty, M. (1978). Effective versus directive style. *Teaching of Psychology, 5*, 193-194.

Overall, J. U., & Marsh, H. W. (1980). Students' evaluations of instruction: A longitudinal study of their stability. *Journal of Educational Psychology, 72*(3), 321-325.

Pasen, R. M., Frey, P. W., Menges, R. J., & Rath, G. (1978). Different administrative directions and student ratings of instruction: Cognitive vs. affective effects. *Research in Higher Education, 9*(2), 161-167.

Seldin, P. (1992). *Evaluating teaching: New lessons learned.* Keynote address presented at "Evaluating Teaching: More Than a Grade" conference held at the University of Wisconsin-Madison, sponsored by the University of Wisconsin System, Undergraduate Teaching Improvement Council.

Seldin, P. (1993). How colleges evaluate professors, 1983 vs. 1993. *AAHE Bulletin, 46*(2), 6-8, 12.

Sixbury, G. R., & Cashin, W. E. (1995). Description of database for the IDEA Diagnostic Form. *IDEA Technical Report No. 9.* Manhattan, KS: Kansas State University, Center for Faculty Evaluation and Development.

Spear, K. (1984). Editor's notes. In K. I. Spear (Ed.), *Rejuvenating introductory courses* (pp. 1-9). San Francisco: Jossey-Bass.

Stevens, J. J. (1987). Using student ratings to improve instruction. In K. M. Aleamoni (Ed.), Techniques for evaluating and improving instruction (pp. 33-38). *New Directions for Teaching and Learning, 31.* San Francisco: Jossey-Bass.

Theall, M. Franklin, J. & Ludlow, L. H. (1990). *Attributions and retributions: Student ratings and the perceived causes of performance*. Paper presented at the annual meeting of the American Educational Research Association, Boston, MA.

The Mystery Shopper Program: An Innovative Tool for Assessing Performance

Charles Schroeder

The first step in any good assessment program is to clarify what matters—what do people really care about? Assessment is not simply a process to gather data and return "results," but rather it is a process that starts with the questions of decision makers, that involves them in systematically gathering and interpreting data, and then informs and helps guide continuous improvement (AAHE, 1992). Staff in the department of Campus Dining Services (a department providing comprehensive food services in five residential dining halls, two student union food courts and three convenience stores) worked for months to develop a strategic plan that included clear performance standards for each unit. Once the standards were established, all staff members underwent intensive training to ensure that they could consistently meet the standards. Although a variety of assessment techniques are used to provide frequent feedback for performance improvement, none is more important than the Mystery Shopper Program. The program has two basic objectives: (a) to provide feedback to units so that progress and critical satisfaction areas can be recorded in order to identify areas that need improvement and (b) to provide feedback to the department management to ensure that all units are making progress in areas identified as critical to the department's long-term success.

How Does the Mystery Shopper Program Work?

Approximately 12 students have been hired and trained to "shop" in CDS operations and observe/critique certain areas. Mystery Shoppers are compensated one-half hour per shop at $5.25 per hour out of the department's marketing budget. The cost of items purchased and/or meals consumed are absorbed by the location receiving the Mystery Shopper's services. Shoppers are primarily recruited by ads placed in the student newspaper and through contacts with faculty in marketing-related majors. One mystery shopper visit per week provides each unit with enough data points to track progress and enables weekly feedback at unit meetings. Each mystery shopper visits four specific units per week at specific time intervals. These assessments focus not only on the content of information the department wants but also on the

75

information the individual units need to be successful. Department-wide shops often focus on such issues as product availability and the degree to which students are pleasantly greeted at all times. Shops in unit-specific areas, however, usually focus on the condition of products and facilities.

Mystery Shoppers use a one-page form with specific questions and room for additional comments. The form is completed within 24 hours of each shop and sent electronically to the CDS marketing department. In order to track the progress of the units, the responses on the mystery shopper forms are entered into a spreadsheet and tallied. Also, a sheet is used to record the logistics of the mystery shopper forms coming into the department to ensure the integrity of the program and shoppers. Most forms, for example, have 14 questions, including items such as: "Were you pleasantly greeted by all employees you encountered?"; "Was the floor clean?"; "Were magazines neatly arranged in the sales rack?"; "Were all employees in uniform with name tags?"; "Were tables being cleaned as customers left?"; "Was the salad bar being kept clean and well-stocked?"; "Were you served in less than two minutes at every station?"; "What food/beverage items did you purchase? Describe your satisfaction with these products (e.g., temperature, freshness, taste, appearance)"; and "Did advertised price points match what you were charged?" Examples of comments from two recent shops are as follows:

> "Food was excellent! Thumbs up for this one. Everything was magnificent. Even the soup was piping hot. Baby carrots were cooked to perfection, still retained firmness also."

> "I had a very pleasant visit at TA Brady's. The food was definitely up to standards. Neither of the two employees had nametags. I wish they were wearing nametags, because they both deserved credit for their job well done. The only thing that needed to be cleaned was the display glass by the sandwich condiments."

How Is the Information Used to Improve Performance?

Supervisors use positive findings from shops to provide immediate feedback (within two days) to employees about what was observed. Supervisors also use positive feedback to recognize staff as a group and to analyze why the activity was so successful. They also use any negative findings generated from shops to improve individual performance. Supervisors, in this case, meet with the individual staff member in private and/or have the staff team handle the issue as a group. In both cases a plan is generated for correcting flaws and improving performance.

Has the Mystery Shopper Program Been Successful?

The Mystery Shopper Program has proven to be an incredibly valuable assessment tool for Campus Dining Services for several reasons. First, it gives the unit team feedback from the customer's point of view. Second, the feedback is specific and focuses on operational performance targets. Third, the feedback is on a regular basis because operations are "shopped" at minimum every other week while most are shopped each week. Finally, the operational performance targets are known to unit team members, so there is no "mystery" about the shops. Team members know the shops will occur—they just do not know by whom and when.

The program has also made other valuable contributions to the department. For example, the open-ended comments allow shoppers to offer suggestions and thoughts based on the customer's perspectives. The positive feedback also bolsters staff pride and reinforces things that are being done effectively.

Although the Mystery Shopper Program has proved to be an invaluable assessment tool for Campus Dining Services, it is not without its challenges. The first challenge encountered was the actual establishment and implementation of the program. In the initial stages, it was very important to include all staff in developing the concept, the objectives/targets to be measured, the form to be used, the method of shopper feedback, and the way the information would be used to improve performance. In addition, each year new shoppers must be selected, trained, and "maintained" with ongoing communications. Finally, since shoppers are expected to submit reports within 24 hours via e-mail, reports must be "tracked" and the results of shops recorded in a timely and systematic fashion. Supervisors, in turn, use the results to ask two fundamental questions: (a) "What is working well?" and (b) "What needs to be changed?"

The Mystery Shopper Program highlights two additional central assumptions about assessment. First, assessment obviously requires attention to outcomes, but it also requires an equal amount of attention to the experiences leading to those outcomes. Second, assessment works best when it is ongoing, not episodic (AAHE, 1992). Clearly, performance improvement is fostered best when assessment entails a linked series of activities undertaken over time. In this regard, the Mystery Shopper Program is one of many assessment tools used by departments within the Division of Student Affairs at the University of Missouri-Columbia. Information gleaned from various "shops" has proven to be invaluable in improving the performance of not only individual staff members but also of units in the department as a whole. And, most importantly, shops have led to substantial increases in student satisfaction with a variety of services and programs.

Can the Mystery Shopper Program Be Used in Other Settings?

The Mystery Shopper Program is easily adaptable to a variety of institutional service areas such as registration, admissions, academic support services, and residence halls. As with the Campus Dining Services example, the key to a successful program is having well established and clear standards; training programs that enable employees to understand and meet the standards; and a small group of mystery shoppers who are trained to observe, record, and communicate the results of their "shops." In addition, certain aspects of the Mystery Shopper Program can be applied to classroom activities. At Penn State University, for example, certain classes have used "quality circles" composed of small groups of students. These "circles" usually involve four to five students who meet frequently to discuss different aspects of the class—what is going well and what could be improved. Members of the circle also poll other members of the class to obtain suggestions for improvements. Circle members then share their observations and feedback on a regular basis with the instructor. A similar program has been in place for over 10 years at Brigham Young University where numerous students are trained to make observations about various dimensions of the class and provide feedback, on a regular and systematic basis, to the professors. Finally, St. John Fisher College has implemented a new program for helping students make the shift from being passive recipients of knowledge to being active partners in their own learning.

Student Management Teams (SMTs) composed of small groups of student volunteers act as liaisons between students in the class and the professor. Team members are responsible for meeting with the professor outside of class to provide feedback gathered through weekly meetings which routinely occur during the first few minutes of the class and provide all students an opportunity to comment on the class material and any other issues of concern. These activities enable SMT members to shape the evolution of course content, structure, and process (Scarcia-King & Sadauskas-Harmon, 1998).

Although there is certainly no "mystery" in these programs, the approach does illustrate the importance of working with faculty to understand their expectations and to reach consensus on the dimensions of the classroom experience they want to target for student feedback. For example, faculty may ask student observers to provide feedback on issues such as: "Are my expectations clear?"; "Am I communicating effectively?"; "Am I providing adequate time for questions and dialogue?"; "Are my learning objectives clear and understandable?"; and "Are my testing procedures encouraging the intended kinds of learning?" Although faculty have known for years the importance of feedback in the learning process for their students, they have often not considered the important role of feedback in improving their teaching and the quality of the learning environment in their classroom. A modified Mystery Shopper Program that focuses on defining clear learning outcomes, identifying methods for achieving those outcomes, and educating student "observers" to record and report their observations could have a dramatic impact on the quality of the classroom learning environment. Readers interested in exploring these options should contact colleagues in their faculty development programs.

Conclusion

Institutions nationwide are increasingly expected to demonstrate accountability for their programs and services. Innovative assessment tools such as the Mystery Shopper Program can provide faculty and staff with ongoing and systematic feedback that not only improves performance, but also often enhances morale, teamwork, satisfaction, and unit cohesion.

References

American Association for Higher Education (AAHE). (1992). *Principles of good practice for assessing student learning*. Washington, DC: Author.

Scarcia-King, T. J., & Sadauskas-Harmon, P. (1998). Student management teams: Helping students take ownership of their classes. *About Campus, 3*, 26-27.

Retention Research with a National Database

Stephen R. Porter

As Peter Ewell mentioned in his remarks elsewhere in this collection, accountability demands from state legislatures and accreditation bodies have been increasing. Although many practitioners in assessment have turned to measures based on survey research, external actors such as state legislatures and the media continue to focus on "hard" outcomes such as retention and graduation rates.

When an institution has a low retention rate, the implication is that many of its students are dropping out. Yet many of these so-called dropouts (or more accurately, stopouts) are actually transfer students. Distinguishing between the two is quite important, as an institution can legitimately argue that its retention rate should be revised to include these transfer-out students. This is especially true for community colleges, with their stated mission to promote the transfer of their students to four-year institutions.

Until recently administrators and researchers have faced a difficult task when trying to distinguish stopouts from transfer-outs. One solution involves using transcript requests to call potential transfer institutions to confirm student enrollment, a time-consuming and possibly expensive strategy. A second solution is to use the data collected by state higher education organizations, but these data sets often do not contain information on private schools and obviously do not include data from out-of-state institutions.

The National Student Clearinghouse (NSC) now offers a service called "Enrollment Search" that provides another way to track transfer-out behavior (see their web site for more information). The NSC has built a database of student enrollments throughout the country based on its student loan reporting service. For a fee (at the time of this publication, 10 cents times an institution's total fall headcount enrollment), a college can submit a list of students who are no longer enrolled at their institution and discover if they are enrolled in another institution in the NSC database. The college will receive information as to whether the student appears in the NSC database at another institution, and if so, the name and FICE code of the transfer institution along with the date of enrollment. In order to participate in the Enrollment Search service, the institution must already be a member of the NSC.

Currently the NSC estimates that about 80% of the students enrolled in postsecondary institutions in the U.S. appear in their database. Coverage rates vary quite a bit by state, ranging from almost zero coverage in Puerto Rico and Hawaii to almost 100% in Kentucky and Utah.   A list of participating schools in each state is available on the NSC web site.

As many of you may know, the NSC has experienced some problems with the Family Educational Rights and Privacy Act (FERPA) and their attempt to provide transfer student data to their member institutions under their former "Transfer Track" program.   The Enrollment Search program has been redesigned to overcome those problems and the Department of Education has stated that the program is in compliance with FERPA.

Even if your state higher education organization collects data on transfer behavior within your state, you may still want to consider using the NSC data to supplement your state data. Karl Boughan (2001) at Prince George's Community College in Maryland used the NSLC data to recalculate the transfer-out rate at his institution. Using state data from the Maryland Higher Education Commission (MHEC), the transfer rate for one cohort after five years was 13%; combining the state data with the NSC data increased the transfer rate six percentage points to 19%. About half of this increase was from students transferring to an out-of-state institution or an institution within Maryland that does not report data to MHEC.

Interestingly, the other half of the increase was due to MHEC's definition of a transfer student. Students are defined as transfers by the state if they enroll with twelve college credits or more (excluding advanced placement credits). So quite a few students would take two or three courses at Prince George's and then enroll at another college, but because of the state's definition they slipped under the radar and were not reported as transfer students to the state's transfer student database.

Once you obtain data from the NSC, it can be used in several different ways. The simplest is to take your stopout rate and determine how many of your stopouts are actually transfer-outs. For example, the 1996 cohort of first-time, full-time degree-seeking first-year students at the University of Maryland, College Park, has a one-year retention rate of 87.4%. Of the 12.6% of the cohort normally labeled as stopouts, the NSC data revealed that 40% of this group were actually transfer-outs (Porter, in press). (This is, of course, an underestimate, since the less than 100% national coverage of the NSC data results in some true transfer-outs being classified as stopouts.) Retention rates can then be recalculated to include this transfer-out component.

The transfer institution data can also be taken into account when calculating transfer-out rates. Transfer behavior is often viewed quite differently at the two-year and four-year levels. For a community college, transferring is generally viewed as good—one of the main functions of the community college is to provide an avenue for students to obtain a baccalaureate degree.

For four-year institutions, however, transferring can be seen as a negative outcome, because students are in essence rejecting their home institution to graduate at another. This may not necessarily be the case at all four-year institutions, especially if students are transferring to a more competitive institution. The FICE codes provided by the NSLC can be used to differentiate between different types of transfer institutions (Porter, 2001).

Finally, the NSLC data can be used to refine statistical models of retention behavior, where outcomes can be defined as trichotomous (stay, transfer, or stopout) rather than the traditional dichotomous outcome (stay versus go). Such a formulation can yield substantively different results from traditional retention models (Porter, in press).

The use of regional and national databases in retention research can yield rich dividends. Retention and graduation rates are still considered basic benchmarks of institutional performance, and these databases can assist institutional researchers and assessment specialists in understanding why students leave their institution. Distinguishing between students who transfer and those who drop out can allow researchers to search for commonalities within the two groups, and lead to retention programs tailored to the specific needs of both groups.

References

Boughan, K. (2001). *Not all transfers are created equal: Some methodological considerations in using National Student Clearinghouse Enrollment Search data.* Paper presented at the Transfer: The Forgotten Function of Community Colleges Conference, Overland Park, KS.

Porter, S. R. (in press). Including transfer-out behavior in retention models: Using the NSC Enrollment Search data. *AIR Professional File.*

Porter, S. R. (2001, February). *Understanding retention outcomes: Using multiple data sources to distinguish between dropouts, stopouts and transfer-outs.* Paper presented at the Second National Forum on First-Year Assessment, Houston, TX.

The Role of Students in Assessment

Catherine A. Palomba   Several contributors in this collection have pointed out that assessment information is not very useful if it does not affect decision making. Others have noted the value of collaboration and how important it is for successful assessment. The topic I address here is how to engage students in our assessment efforts, both as users of the information we produce and as collaborators in the efforts to produce it. Specifically I raise the question of how students can benefit from assessment information, and I offer some suggestions for involving students in the assessment process.

When we design assessment projects, we expect students to help generate assessment information. Students participate in classroom activities, prepare portfolios, take tests, complete inventories, fill out surveys, and share their opinions in focus groups. They provide evidence of their learning, reflections on their growth, and opinions about campus life. All of us who practice assessment hope to use results to improve our programs for future students. But how can we improve the learning of current students? That is, how can we make assessment information immediately useful to the students who help us gather it? One possibility is to provide feedback to students about their assessment efforts and results. A number of assessment experts have argued persuasively for the use of feedback, whether assessing learning in general education, the major, or first-year communities.

Grant Wiggins has been one of the most effective voices in arguing for the use of feedback as a way to improve student learning. Wiggins (1998) believes that assessment should teach as well as measure and that it should provide "rich and useful feedback to all students and to their teachers" (p. 12). One of the strongest trends in assessment is to embed the collection of information about learning into everyday classroom activities. When we do this, the collection of assessment information for programmatic purposes is not obvious to students (although they should be told if the information is going to be used this way.) Because embedded assessment activities are seen as a natural part of the learning process, issues of student motivation are minimized. In addition, many opportunities to provide feedback about learning are available. Wiggins argues that feedback is most

83

effective if it occurs along with assessment activities providing commentary that is "rich, clear, and direct enough" to help students self-assess and correct their performance (p. 12). He urges us to assess how well students are able to use the feedback they receive. Because they often include small classes and connected learning, first-year learning communities offer many opportunities for faculty and staff to provide feedback to students about valued educational outcomes such as critical thinking and communication.

Out-of-class activities such as service learning also benefit if we provide students with feedback and opportunities for self-assessment. According to Barbara Jacoby (1996), service learning is based on the principle that learning and development occur "as a result of a reflective component explicitly designed" to foster this growth (p. 6). Jacoby believes that reflection on service learning can be as important as the experience itself. She argues for many forms of reflection including individual and group, as well as oral and written, and believes that program leaders, peers, and the individuals who are served should provide feedback. Despite the emphasis on classroom assessment, the techniques popularized by Tom Angelo and Patricia Cross (1993) include many strategies that can be adapted for use with out-of-class learning as well.

Students should receive feedback when they complete tests or instruments such as Kolb's Learning Style Inventory or the Defining Issues Test (recommended by Nancy Evans elsewhere in this collection). Students can be given a score sheet containing their individual results along with some explanation of what the results mean for them. Students also appreciate receiving national norms and/or group averages from local test takers.

Providing feedback about in- and out-of-class learning activities seems like a natural thing to do. But how do we provide feedback when the assessment technique we have chosen is a survey of student attitudes and experiences? We have implemented several approaches at Ball State University. One is to gather together some of the highlights of several assessment projects (including surveys and tests) in a brochure called "Expressions." Assessment findings are organized around topics such as choosing Ball State, interacting with faculty, continuing to learn, and expressing satisfaction. Each topic area includes three or four specific findings. For example, under the heading of "continuing to learn," the brochure indicates that "more than 40 percent of entering freshmen would like to get a graduate or professional degree in the future." The brochure is sent to all first-year students so that they can have an idea of what their peers are like and to faculty and staff so that they can have an idea of what matters to their students. Putting assessment results on the web can serve similar purposes.

The Making Achievement Possible (MAP) Survey that we administer to entering first-year students provides an unusual way of sharing individual feedback. Each student who completes MAP receives a personalized report with specific messages that are based on his/her own responses to survey questions. For example, students who express some reservations about how well they are adjusting to campus life are advised to take advantage of a number of campus services, students who plan inadequate study time are advised to study more, and those who have not allocated time for getting involved are urged to take advantage of what the campus has to offer. The personalized report is generated through the use of SPSS and Microsoft Word. It contains graphs and charts as well as narrative and, depending on the specific set of messages, is six to eight pages in length. The report is returned to the student within a day or two of completing the survey. Short reports containing the student's answers are also shared with the academic advisor and residence hall director. The project is a collaborative effort of Academic Assessment, Academic Advising, Residence Life, and the Learning Center. Sherry Woosley, Research Analyst in the Offices of Academic Assessment and Institutional Research, is Project Director. Working on the MAP project has been a wonderful way to bring together faculty and staff who are concerned about the first-year experience. All committee members are dedicated to the idea of sharing feedback from MAP with students.

Recently, Sherry Woosley and Amanda Knerr, an assessment intern from BSU's graduate program in student affairs administration, conducted a focus group with students to get their reactions and suggestions about the MAP student report. One student indicated the report was "uncomfortably accurate" in pinpointing areas of concern. Another felt the report should caution students about spending so much time playing on the computer. Although several students found the report (and the survey) rather long, they asked us to include more specific suggestions about how to respond to adjustment issues identified in the report. The students indicated they liked seeing the comparative information that the report provided about the entire class. They also liked the chance to win a free semester of books (provided to three randomly selected survey respondents).

The focus group example above illustrates the second point I want to make in my remarks. Students can contribute to the assessment process in a wide variety of ways. Many campuses include institution-wide assessment committees, assessment project committees, or advisory committees for first-year learning communities. Among other things, students who serve on these committees can help to articulate learning and development goals for the first year and to identify indicators of a successful first-year experience (such as interactions with faculty and staff or time spent studying with other students in first-year communities.) To evaluate learning goals or determine performance on indicators, students can help design assessment instruments such as tests, portfolios, or surveys.

Several assessment techniques, such as surveys, interviews, and focus groups, offer a way for students to act as assessors of various aspects of the first-year experience—to provide feedback to us. For example, focus groups provide a useful way for students to comment about and make suggestions for improvement in their learning experiences. At Ball State, first-year students have participated in focus groups that addressed how well general education courses were helping students meet the learning goals of the program. At Virginia Commonwealth University students in English classes have written critiques about various aspects of their first year (Fuhrmann, 1995). Students also act as assessors when they evaluate their own work or that of their peers. Evaluating group-work experiences is another example of how students can act as assessors.

Students can assist with the implementation of assessment projects. For example, students can take notes in focus groups or help conduct telephone surveys of other students. In their book, *Assessment in Student Affairs*, Lee Upcraft and John Schuh (1996) include an example from the University of Massachusetts, Amherst where students called "pulsers" regularly conduct telephone surveys on issues of importance to the campus (p. 42). Upper division students can act as coaches for entering students who are participating in performance assessment or portfolio projects. Students can help interpret assessment results. In focus, discussion, or advisory groups, students can be asked to think about what survey results mean or why test results are not what we expected.

Students who participate in focus groups like the one that evaluated the MAP report are actually helping to assess an assessment instrument. Faculty who conduct portfolio projects often ask students to comment on the usefulness of the experience. Students can also evaluate the assessment process as a whole by commenting on its organization and usefulness. As Trudy Banta and I argue in *Assessment Essentials* (1999), involving students is only one of several strategies that are necessary for successful assessment. But, because it is so important, we should look for more opportunities to treat students as partners in the assessment process.

References

Angelo, T. A., & Cross, K. P. (1993). *Classroom assessment techniques: A handbook for college teachers.* (2nd ed.) San Francisco: Jossey-Bass.

Fuhrmann, B. S. (1995). Campus strategies. The prompts project prompts academic and student affairs collaboration. *Assessment Update, 7*(6), 10.

Jacoby, B. (1996). Service-learning in today's higher education." In B. Jacoby & Associates (Eds.), *Service-learning in higher education: Concepts and practices.* San Francisco: Jossey-Bass.

Palomba, C. A., & Banta, T. W. (1996). *Assessment essentials: Planning, implementing, and improving assessment in higher education.* San Francisco: Jossey-Bass.

Upcraft, M. L., & Schuh, J. H. (1996). *Assessment in student affairs: A guide for practitioners.* San Francisco: Jossey-Bass.

Wiggins, G. (1998). *Educative assessment: Designing assessments to inform and improve student performance.* San Francisco: Jossey-Bass, 1998.

Closing the Loop: Assessment Data for Decision Makers

**Kinney Baughman &
Randy L. Swing**

In the preface, John Gardner encourages higher educators to seek greater understanding of the characteristics of entering students and the outcomes created by our programs and policies. As part of that charge he asks, "How are you using [assessment data] to influence institutional decision making and resource allocation?" Unfortunately, the findings of a national study conducted by Peterson, Augustine, and Einarson (2000) found only a minority of institutions could report that assessment had influenced resource allocation or policy. The ideal assessment effort would influence policy and resource allocation by "closing the loop," with a process which identifies what we desire to have happen (our mission/goals), measures what did happen, evaluates the actual outcomes, and informs policy/programming to improve our ability to make the desired outcomes become reality. Implied in this cycle is that assessment data must be available to decision makers in a highly usable form—a condition that in fact is not at all common. How to disseminate data and findings needs to be as carefully considered as any other aspect of first-year program assessment. What is measured, how it is measured and evaluated, and how results are disseminated influence the ultimate effectiveness of the assessment process. Two mistakes in data reporting often serve as the "rule" rather than the "exception." The first mistake is to create data overload. Massive reports or, worse yet, undigested computer printouts of frequency counts prove unhelpful to most administrators, faculty, or staff members. The second mistake is to reduce data so severely that individuals cannot determine how their own actions/decisions are connected to the measured phenomenon. Reports built on "the average student" often mask too much information about the real range of outcomes.

Needed is a method of presenting assessment data that empowers administrators, teachers, and staff to "drill down into the data" or focus on the data most relevant to them at the greatest level of specificity possible. If assessment data is to affect the lived experiences of first-year students, it must be disaggregated to the class, program, or department level. Such efforts, however, could easily overwhelm assessment dissemination efforts. The key is to create data distribution methods that empower users to customize the way they view assessment information.

The plain, hard fact of the matter is that accessing the kind of data with which the assessment professional deals everyday requires the learning of rather sophisticated "data mining" tools such as SPSS, Dbase, or Microsoft Access. However, most end users—that is, administrators, teachers, and staff personnel—have neither the desire nor the time to learn such sophisticated software. Thus, the problem of dissemination boils down to being able to harness the power of a database management system while delivering it to the average user in a manner that, while flexible enough to meet a wide variety of needs, is nevertheless unthreatening, easy to use, and requires a minimal learning curve. Fortunately, a database-enabled web site is a tool that achieves this end.

The heart and soul of the database-enabled web site is the database server. The interface or front-end to the database is the web browser. The glue that binds the two together is a common gateway interface (CGI) program that runs on the web server machine and reports the output of queries to the user's web browser. An example of a database-enabled web site of this type can be found at Appalachian State University's Institutional Research web site. The site provides a set of menus from which the user can choose various reports. The types of reports were selected after several consultations between personnel in the Office of Institutional Research and someone proficient in the construction of online databases. During those meetings the site designers learned that, broadly speaking, most administrators would likely be interested in three categories of reports:

1. *Simple reports.* These reports might display results on how an individual department fared on a survey for any particular year not compared against any other department or college or any other year. Such reports might be of interest to department chairs or program administrators.
2. *Comparative analysis reports.* Department chairs, unit heads, deans, and upper administration personnel may be interested in comparing outcomes between and among departments and/or programs. Such reports would provide a picture of (a) how a particular department stacked up against any other department in the college, (b) how a particular department stacked up against the average scores for the college, and (c) how both departments and colleges stacked up against totals for the university as a whole.
3. *Trend analysis reports.* All administrators would be interested in important trends that might be developing in a department, a college, or the entire university across a number of years.

Having decided which reports were most important, the programmer worked to develop a simple method for allowing the administrators to choose the kind of report they wished to view and to select units for comparison.

On the Appalachian State site, the user encounters a web page containing a menu of possible report types. After selecting a report type, another web page offers drop-down boxes from which to choose the comparison unit of interest and year or years of interest. The payback for this approach to presenting assessment data is twofold. First, each decision presented to the administrator is straightforward. So while the confusion level for the administrator is held to a minimum, the ability to retrieve detailed reports upon which informed decisions can be made is not sacrificed in the least. Second, since every answer leads to another question, institutional researchers are relieved of running countless reports for numerous deans, department chairs, and administrators. Instead, these tasks can be automated to conserve valuable staff time and resources.

The above discussion paints in very broad strokes the approach we took in publishing the Senior Survey results at Appalachian State University. It is intended as an overview of the possibilities of a database-enabled web site. For readers who wish more details, the following section provides a review of the technical aspects of this process.

Creating A Database-Enabled Web Site: The Nuts and Bolts

The database server is the base component of the database-enabled web site. The most popular type of database on the web today is the relational database management system. The language for accessing data in a relational database is SQL. Originally created by IBM, many vendors have since developed their own particular versions of SQL. Different versions generally function alike in the basic "select," "insert," "update," or "delete" statements. A passing knowledge of these four statements will suffice for 90% of all queries one needs for creating dynamic pages on a web site.

Oracle is probably the most recognized name in the SQL/relational database world, but it is far from the only system, much less the most widely used. Readers are encouraged to consider using an alternative program, MySQL, which is available for free as long as the end product is not packaged into a commercial product. The free version and program guide books easily support the needs of a novice user, but company support is also available for more advanced needs when the program is purchased for a very reasonable $150.00.

SQL, like the old MS-DOS operating system, was developed before the advent of Graphical User Interfaces (GUI); thus, SQL commands are typed out at a command line prompt. While typing and learning commands may seem old-fashioned and time consuming, it also offers programmers a great advantage in that they can easily copy and paste commands into complex scripts and subscripts (called embedded SQL).

Web pages are the second part a dynamic assessment data display. Originally, HTML, the computer language that controls web pages, was conceived as a means for presenting "static" data such as research papers and the like, to viewers in remote locations connected to the same network. For example, survey results could be displayed as a series of tables. Such an organization would require the user to scroll through screens and screens of data to find the table of interest and would demand that the data analysis produce a huge number of tables with the data sorted and organized in every possible fashion.

A more efficient way to sort through large data sets would allow users to search for just the information desired and to sort it in a customizable fashion. But allowing for searchability moves beyond the mere creation of pre-defined data tables and requires the use of a database program running on the server where the raw data are stored.

CGI is the third aspect of this data display method and serves as the glue that binds the server to the web page. These computer codes provide a method for opening up a "gateway" into a remote computer for the "common" or unprivileged user, enabling an "interface" with other resources on that computer. CGI enables users to retrieve "dynamic" information such as data tailored to a particular individual's request. Being able to open applications, such as database programs, on remote machines, on which we have no user accounts, is the very reason CGI was invented.

In effect, the CGI program tells the web server software to hand over the "command line" of a remote computer to run "CGI scripts" using input from the user, usually from filling out an HTML form, and to pass this information to a database program like MySQL. MySQL performs sorts, merges, calculations, etc. and hands the results back to the CGI script. The script then writes a virtual HTML page "on the fly" that includes the database output and returns it to the web server software. The server, in turn, sends this "dynamic page" back to the user's browser where it exists for as long as it stays on the user's screen. There is no reason to store such a display permanently as it can be recreated in a matter of seconds of computer time.

If the database server is the heart and soul of the CGI process, the CGI script is the brain. As indicated above, it is the CGI script that bridges the gap between the web server software and the database server. One can write CGI programs in a variety of languages, but two of the most popular scripting languages are Perl and PHP. Both of these languages are free, are open-source, and have large, loyal, and best of all, helpful user bases. A quick search on the Internet will find numerous newsgroups and documents to support the novice or expert user. Most campuses will have at least one technical expert knowledgeable in these computer languages.

Just how does the CGI script glue all these disparate pieces together? It is helpful to think of the CGI script as being a virtual "you." That is, the CGI script reproduces in every respect what you yourself would do if you were sitting at a computer creating a query using MySQL. First, you would either boot up your PC or log into a network machine (telnet schoolmachine.yourschool.edu). Next you would open up a database in MySQL (%mysql mydb). Then you would issue an "I want to find such and such" statement; for example, you could seek a person in an address book (mysql>select firstname,lastname,phonenumber from addressbook where lastname="Swing" and city="Boone"). You would end by reading or recording the results.

There is a Perl counterpart to each one of those commands. Instead of manually doing these steps each time you wish to look up someone's phone number, imagine typing out a little program that was written with a particular HTML form in mind which asks the user: "What is the [Last Name] of the person you're looking for and what [City] does (s)he live in?" This example provides the gist of what is involved in writing a CGI script.

What is particularly gratifying about writing online database programs is the power that comes from using both SQL and Perl together in the production of reports that require quite a lot of number crunching. The reports written for the Department of Institutional Research at Appalachian State University are prime examples. Those pages were created from a dataset containing column after column of rows upon rows of survey data—5's, 4's, 3's, 2's, and 1's representing "strongly agree," "agree," neutral," disagree," and "strongly disagree." Using relatively straightforward SQL statements the program receives total counts for each question, as well as the totals for each answer to that question and stores them all in variables.

(select count(*) from surveyX where question=1 and college="AS") and (select count(*) from surveyX where question=1 and answer=5 and college="AS")

With these two numbers in hand, Perl can be used to compute the percentages for those students in the college of Arts and Sciences (AS) who answered 5 to question number 1. And using HTML, one can write out the total number of responses for Question 1 for Arts and Science students, the total number of answers equal to 5 for Question 1 as well as the percentages stored in a variable before moving on to basically the same routine for the next query.

Thus, using MySQL to retrieve raw data from an electronic dataset, Perl to calculate percentages, and HTML to format the output is a powerful way to present assessment data so that individual users can focus on the data of greatest interest. Data are more powerful and more likely to be used when teachers and administrators are empowered to drill down in datasets and focus on those data of greatest connection to their own work.

References

Peterson, M. W., Augustine, C. H., & Einarson, M. K. (2000). *Organizational practices enhancing the influence of student assessment information in academic decisions.* Paper presented at the annual meeting of the Association for Institutional Research, Cincinnati, OH.

Part 3

Program & Institutional Examples

First-Year Experience Jeopardy

Betsy O. Barefoot

Answer: The Freshman/First-Year Seminar

Question: What is the most frequently assessed course in the college curriculum?

Neither I nor anyone else I know has actually verified the answer to the above question, but I believe it to be true. As many of you know, first-year seminars (i.e., freshman seminars, college success courses) are often implemented because of their reputation for improving retention rates and grade point averages for participating students. In fact, some institutions create these courses believing them to be the magic bullet that single-handedly will solve retention problems and address student academic deficiencies. So determining whether the "first-year seminar magic" happened is a fairly common form of assessment.

In my 11 years as co-director for research and publications at the University of South Carolina's National Resource Center on The First-Year Experience and Students in Transition, one of my assigned projects was compiling institutional research studies on the first-year seminar. With the financial support of the Houghton Mifflin Publishing Company, the Center compiled two volumes entitled *Exploring the Evidence: Reporting Outcomes of First-Year Seminars*. These volumes (which are still available from the National Resource Center) contain brief summaries of approximately 90 institutional research studies—most of them never published in any other form—on seminar outcomes. As you might imagine, research on first-year seminars is of varying quality. Occasionally, a college or university will conduct a tightly controlled, random sample study of seminar effects. But more often, studies compare existing populations of participants and non-participants or matched samples within existing populations. The overwhelming majority of research studies investigate course effects on student retention, fewer look at possible effects on grade point averages, and even fewer focus on other possible learning objectives or changes in behaviors and/or attitudes.

Research Findings

What does the research on first-year seminars find? Before launching into a description and analysis of findings, it's important to acknowledge something my colleague, Dorothy Fidler, editor of the *Journal of The First-Year Experience and Students in Transition*, used to say on a weekly basis—"research isn't perfect." That means that we can rarely, if ever, totally rule out the Hawthorne effect, the volunteer effect, the halo effect, and a whole host of other effects that confound our attempts to understand college student behavior. But we are building a body of research that seems to indicate that first-year seminars are positively correlated with improved student retention. Notice, please, that I didn't say "freshman seminars cause students to be retained." First-year seminars, by design, function as support groups and as a way of introducing students to behaviors that encourage success. There is a predictable, widely found correlation between participation in these small-group courses and the likelihood of "hanging in there" and ultimately graduating. And this positive correlation has been consistent for about 30 years at the few institutions where routine long-term assessment of seminar outcomes has been undertaken. With respect to percentage differences, participation in first-year seminars has been correlated with a 2% to 10% increase in retention—differences which may or may not be statistically significant, depending on the size of the population (Barefoot, 1993; Barefoot, Warnock, Dickinson, Richardson, & Roberts, 1998).

While doubting that a first-year seminar can, all by itself, improve student retention, I do believe, based on my years of evaluating research studies, that these seminars are one weapon in the retention arsenal and, when coupled with other forms of support, can make a critical difference for first-year students. Do first-year seminars always show a positive correlation with retention? The answer is no. But when studies find no effect or even a negative effect, then I start to ask questions about the seminar design—who teaches it, whether instructors have received training or support, whether the class fosters high levels of interaction between participants and instructor, and what is actually being taught.

The evidence linking first-year seminars to improvements in academic achievement is far less consistent. Some courses seem to make a positive difference for some students; other courses seem to have no effect at all, especially with students who have the greatest academic deficiencies (Barefoot, 1993, Kennesaw State University). Actually, when you think about it, students who have seriously inadequate academic backgrounds need far more help than can be provided in any single course that might last for one semester. In a nutshell, improving the academic performance of first-year students is a far more elusive and complicated objective than retaining them.

Other outcomes that research studies have found to be positively correlated with first-year seminars include the following:

- Graduation rates (Barefoot, 1993, University of South Carolina)
- Credit hours attempted/completed (Barefoot, 1993, four North Carolina community colleges)
- Student adjustment and involvement (Barefoot et. al, 1998, University of California, Santa Barbara)
- Student satisfaction (Barefoot et. al, 1998, Idaho State University)
- Student accuracy of self-assessment (Barefoot, 1993, Elmhurst College)
- Changes in students' self-reported sexual decision making (Barefoot, 1993, University of South Carolina)

♦ And last, but certainly not least, changes in faculty attitudes and behaviors as a result of teaching a first-year seminar (Barefoot et. al, 1998, Montana State University, Bozeman)

First-year seminars have been used as the venue for other interesting research such as the effects of gender on seminar instruction (how male/female instructors interact differently with male/female students) (Blackhurst, 1995) and patterns of "student talk" versus "faculty talk" in courses intentionally designed to be highly interactive (Burk, 1997). Additional research has investigated the effect of class size (Barefoot, 1993, North Dakota State University) and has compared the effects of different seminar types on a single campus—i.e., highly academic courses, student success courses, and outdoor experiential courses (Barefoot et. al, 1998, Salisbury State University).

First-year seminars have the distinct advantage of lending themselves to experimental pedagogies. They are free from a rigid adherence to content (there is no "canon" for the first-year seminar) and can focus more on the process of learning. Therefore, these courses have been the site for a rich variety of research studies on student learning, course structure, and instructional method. But few of these studies make it into the published higher education literature. The reasons vary—some of the studies are flawed in one way or another, while others simply never receive the attention it takes to turn raw data into a concise publication. Occasionally research findings do not conform to the public image an institution wishes to portray, so the findings are buried or trashed—even though they could be valuable to the larger higher education community.

Final Comments/Observations

Here are a few final comments and observations for anyone who has administration or evaluation of a first-year seminar in their "portfolio," so to speak.

1. First-year seminars are not a magic bullet that will change student behavior. Seminars can serve as one piece of a comprehensive first-year program—a linchpin of sorts to give coherence to the curriculum and cocurriculum. But if these courses serve as an antidote to the rest of the first-year experience, their effectiveness will always be diluted.

2. First-year seminar effects can be multiplied through connections with other structures and programs such as learning communities, advising, orientation, and residence life.

3. Assessment of course outcomes is important. If seminars are to survive the vicissitudes of changing administrations and fluctuating resources, there must exist some evidence that the course is doing for students and for the institution what it was designed to do.

4. Assessment and course design should proceed simultaneously. An after-the-fact assessment plan is not the way to go. Courses can be designed to achieve certain objectives, but attempting to evaluate a course for which no specific measurable objectives were articulated is tough, to say the least.

Finally, it has been my experience that educators who conduct assessments of first-year seminars are happy to share their research methods, experiences, successes, and problems with anyone who is beginning this process. Both I and my colleagues at the University of South Carolina's National Resource Center for The First-Year Experience and Students in Transition would be happy to put you in touch with others whose institutional profiles and seminar courses are similar to yours.

References

Barefoot, B. (Ed.). (1993). *Exploring the evidence: Reporting outcomes of freshman seminars* (Monograph No. 11). Columbia, SC: National Resource Center for The Freshman Year Experience, University of South Carolina.

Barefoot, B., Warnock, C., Dickinson, M., Richardson, S., & Roberts, M. (Eds.). (1998). *Exploring the evidence: Reporting the outcomes of first-year seminars, Volume II* (Monograph No. 25). Columbia, SC: National Resource Center for The First-Year Experience and Students in Transition, University of South Carolina.

Blackhurst, A. (1995). The relationship between gender and student outcomes in a freshman orientation course. *Journal of The Freshman Year Experience, 7*(2), 63-80.

Burk, T. L. (1997). *Faculty instructional development and oral communication in freshman seminars at the College of William and Mary,* Unpublished doctoral dissertation, College of William and Mary.

Assessing Curricular Learning Communities

Jodi H. Levine

Recently there has been a dramatic increase in the number of campuses offering "learning communities." While this essay addresses assessment in curricular learning communities, it is worthwhile to note some of the different contexts in which the phrase "learning community" is currently applied: (a) individual classrooms, (b) curricular learning communities, (c) virtual learning communities, (d) residential learning communities, (e) communities of faculty, (f) learning communities as "learning organizations," and (g) learning communities in the community development sense. How a campus or organization defines its learning communities directly affects decisions about assessment.

Curricular learning communities can be defined as:

> a variety of approaches that link or cluster classes during a given term, often around an interdisciplinary theme, that enroll a common cohort of students. This represents an intentional restructuring of students' time, credit and learning experiences to foster more explicit intellectual connections between students, between students and their faculty, and between disciplines. (MacGregor, Smith, Matthews, & Gabelnick, 1997)

Regardless of the definition or model that guides your work, a successful evaluation of learning communities will be characterized by three elements: (a) the ability to balance multiple agendas and serve many purposes, (b) a collaborative nature, and (c) the extent to which it is ongoing.

Multi-Purpose in Scope

Jean MacGregor (1995) wrote that an evaluation of learning communities involves balancing two closely related agendas: proving and improving. Evaluation for proving involves recording and describing the impact of learning communities on both internal and external audiences, while evaluation for improving is conducted to gather information for the purposes of problem solving and program improvement.

The research plan for learning communities must be centered on the principle that teaching and learning in these communities occur in a dynamic environment composed of a variety of academic and social interactions. You cannot expect to capture all that is happening in such a community with a single "snap shot" evaluation approach. Nor can a retention or achievement study alone, even if it shows impressive gains, accurately describe what takes place in a learning community classroom. Rather, program evaluators should consider a mixed-method approach, stocking their toolboxes with research methods that can assess both process and outcomes. Further, such evaluative work should assess the impact of the programs not only on students and teachers but also on the institution. What institutional practices or programs (e.g., orientation, placement testing, residential life) have learning communities affected?

The assessment plan should be closely linked to the goals of learning-community efforts. Those involved in assessment should repeatedly ask "Why are we doing this?" as they plan assessment activities. Discussion of the "why" will likely include consideration of both formative (process and improvement) and summative (accountability and feasibility) issues. A comprehensive approach to assessment and a well-executed formative evaluation can yield rich, descriptive information that can also be used for accountability purposes.

Collaborative in Nature

By design, learning communities are a uniting of students, teachers, and disciplines. The most successful learning community programs are those developed in a culture of cross-campus collaboration and consultation. The assessment design should also be collaborative and built out of consensus. Those charged with assessing the learning community program should consider research methods that are more collaborative in nature, such as qualitative approaches, classroom assessment techniques, and action research. Moreover, program stakeholders, particularly teachers and students, should be involved in the planning and implementation of the research agenda. For example, in developing an end-of-semester course evaluation for learning community classes, program evaluators may form an evaluation design group composed of faculty from different disciplines and students of varying ability levels.

On a cautionary note, administrators should be careful not to overstudy program participants. In the early stages of a program the tendency is to constantly observe, survey, and measure what is going on in learning communities. Research activities should be scheduled in a way that is least intrusive on precious teaching and learning time and space.

To streamline the evaluation process, researchers should consider their needs and plans alongside assessment activities already taking place on the campus. There is no need to reinvent the wheel. If your institution already collects and analyzes demographic data on entering students, this information may serve as a baseline for learning community research.

Ongoing

Assessment should not be an afterthought. Assessment plans should be designed alongside other regularly scheduled decisions such as budgeting, course scheduling, marketing, and recruiting. Further, the research plan should be figured into the program budget. Program designers should estimate costs as they weigh the pros and cons of different assessment methods. Regardless of the model or approach, designers should anticipate and plan for the fiscal, human, and technical resources needed to execute the assessment plan. Again, taking an inventory of other assessment projects being conducted on campus in which the program might take part is a smart move. This strategy, while not only cost effective, can also increase program visibility and credibility.

Learning community development occurs in stages: design, implementation, and maintenance. Assessment must take place throughout all three stages and should be cyclical, with results being applied to program improvement. The questions asked during the implementation stage of the work will need to be repeated and reshaped as the program develops. New questions should be asked as more students and teachers participate in and experience learning communities.

Learning communities represent a systematic and comprehensive model for improving teaching and learning, particularly at the undergraduate level. The cross-campus, multi-disciplinary approach to building learning communities should be maintained when it is time to assess and evaluate the project.

References and Additional Resources

Borden, V., & Rooney, P. (1998). Evaluating and assessing learning communities. *Metropolitan Universities, 9*(1), 73-88.

Gabelnick, F., MacGregor, J., Matthews, R. S., & Smith, B. L. (1990). Learning communities: Creating connections among students, faculty, and disciplines. In *New Directions for Teaching and Learning, 41*. San Francisco: Jossey-Bass.

Ketcheson, K., & Levine, J. H. (1999). Evaluating and assessing learning communities. In J. H. Levine (Ed.) *Learning communities: New structures, new partnerships for learning* (Monograph No. 26) (pp. 97-108). Columbia, SC: University of South Carolina, National Resource Center for The First-Year Experience and Students in Transition.

Levine, J., Smith, B. L., & Tinto, V. (1999). *Learning about learning communities: Taking structure seriously.* [Teleconference]. Columbia, SC: University of South Carolina, National Resource Center for The First-Year Experience and Students in Transition.

Love A. G., Russo, P., & Tinto, V. (1995). Assessment of collaborative learning programs: The promise of collaborative research. In Washington Center Evaluation Committee (Ed.) *Assessment in and of collaborative learning: A handbook of strategies*. Olympia, WA: Washington Center for Improving the Quality of Undergraduate Education.

MacGregor, J., Smith, B. L., Matthews, R. S., & Gabelnick, F. (1997, March). *Learning community models*. Paper presented at the National Conference on Higher Education, American Association of Higher Education, Washington, DC.

MacGregor, J. (1995). Going public: How collaborative learning and learning communities invite new assessment approaches. In Washington Center Evaluation Committee (Ed.) *Assessment in and of collaborative learning: A handbook of strategies*. Olympia, WA: Washington Center for Improving the Quality of Undergraduate Education.

Shapiro, N. S., & Levine, J. H. (1999). *Creating learning communities: A practical guide to winning support, organizing for change, and implementing programs*. San Francisco: Jossey-Bass.

IUPUI - University College Assessment

Trudy W. Banta

In his initial invitation to participate in the assessment listserv, John Gardner asked us to "share a range of first-year assessment procedures and tools." This piece highlights several of the strategies we've used at Indiana University-Purdue University Indianapolis (IUPUI).

Over the last four years, IUPUI has established a new University College (UC) to serve as the entry point for all beginning students. Scott Evenbeck, Dean of University College, and UC faculty have been successful in garnering grant support for first-year initiatives. One such initiative is a one-credit first-year seminar connected to an introductory course (part of our learning community program) and accompanied by peer mentoring. Vic Borden, Director of Information Management and Institutional Research, has worked closely with UC faculty to develop a multi-faceted evaluation design to monitor the effectiveness of these approaches. The design includes assessment of student learning and satisfaction with their first-year experiences as well as one-year retention and persistence-to-graduation rates.

We use student records to assess student performance (course grades) and persistence in learning communities. In these analyses, we control for background differences among students who participate and those who do not (using linear regression to control for the impact of such variables as high school percentile rank, credit load, and age).

Through the use of student surveys, we indirectly assess student learning of a set of campus-wide generic outcomes called the Principles of Undergraduate Learning (skills in communicating, thinking critically, integrating and applying knowledge, and understanding diverse societies and cultures). We are also developing direct measures of student learning via electronic portfolios in introductory writing, math, and speech courses.

We use classroom assessment techniques to gauge the effectiveness of peer mentoring. In addition, Faculty Fellows, who are awarded stipends for their work, have undertaken a series of qualitative evaluations of the experiences of students, faculty, and staff who have been engaged in first-year initiatives.

Finally, UC faculty have participated in a consortium of urban institutions working under the auspices of a Pew grant to assess their first-year programs. This project has culminated in a peer review for IUPUI that has produced several important recommendations for improvement that are being implemented.

We have found that participation in both learning communities and peer mentoring produces small, but significant gains in course grades and first-year retention, even after adjusting for background factors. However, these efforts have not yet had a discernible impact on long-term student persistence. In addition, our work indicates that high school percentile rank accounts for 50% of the variance in first-year retention at IUPUI.

Unless or until we substantially increase the average percentile class rank of our entering students—difficult to do when our city and region count on us to keep open a very wide door—all of our good work in the first year is, in all likelihood, not going to make a noteworthy increase in our overall retention rate, the statistic that is of utmost importance to members of our board of trustees.

Given the good data we are collecting—from student records, surveys, classroom assessment techniques, and peer review—we can provide evidence of small gains achieved by our first-year initiatives to date. But colleagues who are not involved in these efforts are asking, "Can we—should we—continue a costly program that makes only a small difference when the campus has large needs in other areas?" Those who are providing the leadership for University College believe that we need a bit more time to continue our first-year initiatives and our assessment efforts in order to build stronger arguments to convince our skeptical colleagues.

Part 4

Conclusions & Recommendations

Highlights from the 1999 and 2000 AAHE Assessment Conferences

Linda Suskie

Recently, I edited *Assessment to Promote Deep Learning* (Suskie, 2001), a collection of major addresses from the 1999 and 2000 American Association for Higher Education (AAHE) Assessment Conferences. These conferences were the 14th and 15th sponsored by the AAHE Assessment Forum. The Forum describes itself as the primary national network connecting and supporting higher education stakeholders involved in assessment. It aims to promote thoughtful, effective approaches to assessment and to help campuses and individuals with assessment efforts.

As I worked on this collection, I was struck by how fortunate we are to have so many dedicated, knowledgeable, well-spoken people working on and thinking about assessment issues. Here, I would like to share some lessons from these addresses that will be of interest to those engaged in the assessment of first-year initiatives.

Learning Communities

Because first-year experience programs are recent innovations at many campuses, approaches to assessing these programs are also fairly new. If I had to choose one keynote presentation as most relevant to those involved in first-year assessment, it would be "Assessment of Innovative Efforts: Lessons from the Learning Community Movement" by Jean MacGregor, Vincent Tinto, and Jerri Holland Lindblad. In their presentation, they share lessons from the learning community movement that can be applied to other innovative programs, like first-year experience initiatives. These lessons include:

- ♦ Program development and assessment must occur simultaneously, and we need to be equally serious about both.
- ♦ Assessments are hard to do well if they do not have clear goals and a clear audience.
- ♦ Gathering data is not as important as using it strategically and communicating it to both receptive and not-so-receptive audiences.

Learning communities are a feature of many first-year programs, so it was gratifying to learn from this presentation that learning community students generally fare better academically, socially, and personally than their peers. This is especially true for at-risk students, underrepresented students, and students who generally earn Cs and Ds. Furthermore, learning community students' learning goes deeper, is more integrated, and is more complex, and participants develop sensitivity to and respect for other points of view, other cultures, and other people.

Student Learning

Keynotes by Noel Entwistle, James Anderson, and Sharon Robinson give valuable advice on how to promote student learning during the first year of college.

Evaluation and the Impact on Student Learning

Because the key aim of assessment is the improvement of student learning, Noel Entwistle, from the University of Edinburgh in Scotland, speaks to strategies for promoting "deep" rather than "surface" learning. In deep or active learning, students relate what they are learning to previous knowledge, look for the "big picture," and examine arguments cautiously and critically. Surface learners, on the other hand, only put forth minimal effort, tend to memorize rather than reflect, and do not take the time to think about why they are learning something or how all the pieces fit together. Research suggests that we can promote deep learning by:

- Making clear to students our overarching goals and aims
- Relating what we are teaching to what students already know
- Teaching so that we clarify meanings and arouse interest
- Encouraging metacognition (i.e., engaging students in thinking not only about what they are learning but how they are learning it)

One of Entwistle's major points is that the assessment tools we choose directly affect how our students learn. For example, students are likely to study for multiple choice tests by memorizing facts but are more likely to study for essay tests and similar assessments using deep learning strategies. How we grade assessments also affects how our students learn. We should give more credit, for example, to a student essay with detailed, structured, independent arguments (i.e., one that demonstrates deep learning) than to one that merely describes what the student has learned (i.e., demonstrating superficial learning). The implication for first-year courses is clear: We need to find ways to move first-year assessments from multiple choice tests to assessments that encourage deep learning.

Learning Styles

Increasingly, educators are realizing that treating students equitably does not mean treating them all the same. Students' backgrounds and temperaments affect how they learn and should, consequently, affect the way we teach. In "Developing a Learning-Style/Teaching-Style Assessment Model for Diverse Populations," James Anderson discusses cultural differences in learning styles. Anderson identifies several conditions for optimal student learning.

- Students need to see the relevance of the material through real-life examples to their own experiences and cultures, an assertion shared by Entwistle.

When they fail to see such relevance, students from diverse backgrounds become distracted and "tune out." When they do see the connection, however, they become more engaged, their learning experience becomes more holistic, and they study harder.

♦ Students learn best when they see the holistic or "big picture" of what they're learning.

♦ Student learning is improved when students care about the instructor and when the instructor expresses confidence in their ability.

♦ Students need to receive feedback that helps them learn about themselves as learners, a strategy that parallels Entwistle's recommended focus on metacognition.

♦ Students learn best when they are in a classroom that is student-oriented and encourages social interaction.

Thus, the huge, anonymous lecture-style classes typical of so many first-year introductory courses are antithetical to what many students need in order to succeed. Anderson's lesson is that we need to find ways to give students, especially at-risk students, these kinds of learning experiences in their first year.

Testing and the Underprepared Student

In "Testing Disadvantaged Students: The Elusive Search for What is Fair," Sharon Robinson addresses the issue of student learning from a somewhat different perspective. She notes that the performance of students is directly related to the quality of education they receive. She suggests that we can help disadvantaged or underprepared students obtain a quality education, and thereby perform optimally on assessments, by following the "three Ts":

♦ *Tell* students what is going to be taught. Involve diverse voices in defining the knowledge that we value, a suggestion seconded by Entwistle.

♦ *Teach* and emphasize the material on which students will be tested. Give every student an opportunity to learn what we value.

♦ *Test* the material that we teach. Ensure that exams are testing the material we intend to test.

The Future of Assessment

A 1999 panel—"Assessment at the Millennium: Now What?" with Tom Angelo, Peter Ewell, and Cecilia Lopez—offers views on what we have learned in the 15-year assessment movement, to which I add thoughts on the implications for first-year assessment:

♦ Start with what you already have. What information does your institution already collect about first-year students and their first-year experiences?

♦ Build on success. What is the most successful aspect of your first-year program? Start by assessing and celebrating it!

♦ Focus assessment on what matters most. Your first-year program probably has too many goals to assess all at once. Start by assessing the goals that are most closely related to your institution's mission and priorities.

- Key stakeholders need to know what is in it for them. Any new initiative— first-year programs, assessment, or anything else—needs the active and enthusiastic support of campus leaders in order to succeed. This support is easier to garner if stakeholders understand the benefits to their individual programs and to the institution as a whole.
- Assessment requires a culture shift, in which it is viewed as a continuous and a scholarly activity. Assessing first-year programs is not a once-and-done activity; it is ongoing, with each new assessment raising new questions.

Where is assessment going from here? The panel identified three forces that will impact assessment in many ways in coming years: (a) accountability demands, (b) the growing diversification of postsecondary education, and (c) the movement toward the student-centered learning paradigm.

I see these forces affecting the first-year experience in direct ways. The continuing shift to the learning paradigm means that the focus on creating an engaged, student-centered campus will continue. First-year experience programs may not only grow and strengthen but may also expand to subsequent years. Meanwhile, I read into the rise in accountability demands and higher education diversification the increasingly strong presence of the for-profit sector. These institutions must demonstrate their effectiveness in order to survive, and their emphasis on assessment will put more pressure on the rest of us—including those involved with first-year programs—to do the same.

References

Suskie, L. (Ed.) (2001). *Assessment to promote deep learning: Insights from AAHE's 2000 and 1999 assessment conferences.* Washington, DC: American Association for Higher Education.

The Jury Is In

John N. Gardner
In the preface to this collection, I described some of the objectives and activities of the Policy Center on the First Year of College funded by The Pew Charitable Trusts, and I specifically made reference to ongoing assessment work involving regional consortia focusing on the first college year. The jury is in from its deliberations, so to speak, and this piece, on one level, will share some conclusions and recommendations that have emerged from this project. But our findings and the resulting recommendations have much in common with what other good thinkers on assessment reported in their postings to the FYA listserv. In that spirit, I will attempt to let the findings from our particular project speak for the larger outcomes reported elsewhere in this publication. I do not intend to have final word here. Ultimately, first-year assessment practitioners and other readers have to draw their own conclusions about the strategies and tools needed to assess the first college year.

It was truly our belief that improving the total quality of the first-year college experience, especially the learning realized by first-time college students, could not be done without more valid information about the real nature of that first-year experience as opposed to what we think students are experiencing.

Towards that end, we created five regional consortia in 1999-2000, that included the following:

1. Fifteen public university campuses in the University System of Georgia, both two-year and four-year
2. Five private campuses in Georgia, all members of the Georgia Association of Independent Colleges and Universities
3. Nine community colleges and one regional comprehensive public university, all members of the Appalachian Learning Alliance spearheaded by Appalachian State University in North Carolina
4. Eleven public institutions (ten four-year and one two-year) in the state of Virginia in a consortium convened by the State Council for Higher Education, Virginia
5. Twenty-two private colleges and universities in North Carolina, all members of the North Carolina Association of Independent Colleges and Universities

Program Overview

Three of these groups held organizational meetings in November and December of 1999 and two more in January 2000. We invited them to join in this strictly voluntary process and informed them that we would reconvene them in June and November 2000 for a day-long meeting to report on their progress and to receive feedback from those of us on the staff.

Each of these institutions started by reviewing *Guidelines for Evaluating the First-Year Experience*, originally written and published in 1990. Individual institutions were not charged with using these guidelines as a mandatory template; instead, they were urged to use them as a catalyst to help decide what questions they wanted to ask to understand better the first-year experience on their campus. We found that a number of the institutions used *Guidelines for Evaluating*, verbatim, others used parts of the booklet, and still others completely set aside *Guidelines for Evaluating* and came up with their own set of questions. The results of this kind of thinking are posted on our web site. We found the questions raised by the campuses to be both fascinating and instructive. For example, a committee from a public regional comprehensive university in Virginia, decided before they could address any questions, which might help them rethink their first-year experience on their campus, they first needed to develop a specific philosophy for what they wanted their institution's first-year experience to be. Another campus, again a public institution in Virginia with an open door admissions policy, decided to address the very fundamental question of whether a correlation existed between attendance in classes and academic success. This led the institution to reexamine its attendance policy, an issue pursued only with great reluctance by faculty on most campuses. It is important to note that this examination process enabled institutions to study some of the questions central to producing successful learning in the beginning college experience.

As a result of the feedback we received on the use of *Guidelines for Evaluating*, the booklet has been revised and published by the National Resource Center for The First-Year Experience and Students in Transition in two new editions, one for use in two-year colleges and universities and the other for use in four-year colleges and universities. At the time of this writing, we have two more consortia underway in Alabama and Mississippi. We invite future users of *Guidelines for Evaluating* and this process to share their findings, recommendations, and activities with us. This is definitely ongoing assessment work—a work in progress. What follows are my conclusions from our first use of *Guidelines for Evaluating* in assessment practice.

Conclusions and Recommendations

Successful first-year assessment initiatives generally have grass-roots ownership, the support of senior campus administrators, cross-divisional participation, and student involvement.

We recommend that institutions create a campus-wide, cross-functional group to monitor the first college year on an ongoing basis. Higher education culture usually creates permanent structures, especially faculty committees, to provide oversight and guidance for those areas of college life deemed to be the most important. The initial college experience is critical to the subsequent success of all

students and for an institution to achieve the goals implicit in its mission statement. Given the importance of the first year, we believe that each institution would
be well served by having a permanent group not only conduct an initial assessment of the first college year, but also continue this process on an ongoing basis.
With respect to the composition of these ongoing cross-functional groups, we
strongly recommend that they be composed of these key constituencies: faculty,
academic administrators, staff, student affairs officers, institutional research/self-
study personnel, and students. While the key stakeholders listed above are frequently called on to participate in first-year assessment initiatives, we have found
that institutions almost never include institutional research and self-study staff in
these working groups.

Involving the chief academic officer in assessment work is important.
    In our work with these consortia, we found that campuses that seemed to
make the most progress during the six to nine months of this voluntary assessment
process were those institutions that had a chief academic officer involved in some
meaningful way in that process. We recommend those who would replicate this
process intentionally include the chief academic officer and assign a significant
role to this individual.

Broad-based assessment of the first year as a unit of analysis is rare.
    Institutions should treat the first year as a unit of analysis. What most cam-
puses do instead is break the first-year experience down into a number of discreet
elements. I refer to this as differentiating the forest from the trees. For example, a
campus will assess the ability levels of entering students in such areas as reading,
writing proficiency, mathematical skills, and computer literacy and then attempt to
measure gains in these areas over time. We do not believe this tells us much about
how the efforts of students to improve their academic abilities may or may not be
related to other elements of the college experience that transcend the classroom.

Retention is the overwhelming focus of first-year assessment.
    Outcome measures should encompass a broad vision of the first year that is
consistent with an institution's mission and definition of student success. This is
not in any way to denigrate the significance of retention, but it is to say that the
outcomes implicit in institutional mission statements are ultimately the most important ones we need to connect to the nature of the first college year. In their way,
these goal statements become the basis for assessing the senior year, with the first-
year serving as a kind of baseline.

Most existing assessments of first-year outcomes are quantitative.
    First-year assessment should combine a variety of data collection methods
and include both quantitative and qualitative findings. In order to understand the
student experience, it is essential that students be represented, literally, in this assessment process. Students have stories to tell, and they want to tell them. We
recognize the immediate attractiveness of objective and empirical student data,
but we strongly believe this must be complemented by qualitative findings.

Many readily available data sources are not used in first-year assessment efforts.
    Elsewhere in this collection, noted assessment researcher Peter Ewell has ar-
gued that campuses should conduct a "data audit." They should work to inventory

and connect existing data on first-year students. For example, there are many campus offices that collect data on students related to the specific functional responsibility of their area, such as the library, campus police, health center, student discipline office, or registrar. Unfortunately, these offices rarely share their information, and there is almost never any campus-wide effort to collect, integrate, and synthesize all of these data to represent a coherent, more sophisticated understanding of who the students actually are. Recognizing the need for a model of such a data audit, the Policy Center has in development with Peter Ewell and the National Center for Higher Education Management Systems (NCHEMS) exactly such a template. This will be piloted in Fall 2001 and will be available for general dissemination to and use by interested institutions in 2002.

First-year programs are more likely to be sustained if they include assessment; however, assessment of first-year programs is often an afterthought.

From the beginning, assessment should be incorporated into program planning and development. One of the most powerful lessons I have learned is that many of the archetypal first-year "innovative" programs—like learning communities and first-year seminars—are much more likely to survive if they have assessment data to demonstrate that they are indeed achieving their objectives. Indeed, I believe the ability to present tangible evidence of desired outcomes has been the key to the expansion and continued support of the first-year seminar at the University of South Carolina. For a quarter of a century this program has engaged in ongoing assessment, directed by an individual who is completely independent of the program and who is highly regarded by faculty and staff alike for his research skills and his intellectual and personal integrity. This kind of assessment is even more necessary in times of economic downturn, when tough questions are asked about which first-year initiatives to enhance, maintain, or discontinue.

First-year baseline data are the foundation for value-added assessment.

Data collection at point of entry is a critical first step in evaluating the undergraduate experience. To help institutions achieve this goal, the Policy Center has been working with the Higher Education Research Institute at the University of California, Los Angeles to develop a specific instrument that will collect data at the end of the first college year. We titled this instrument, Your First College Year, and have developed it as a post-test to the well known national survey instrument, The Annual Freshman Survey, an integral component of the Cooperative Institutional Research Program. Thanks to CIRP, we have had for more than three decades, a detailed portrait of what American college students (especially full-time, traditional age students) are like at the time of matriculation. We have not been able to assess, however, what kind of change they may or may not have made over the first college year. By Spring 2002, we will have conducted a series of pilot administrations of this new instrument. More information on the instrument and our findings is available on the Policy Center web site.

First-year assessment is not sufficiently connected with institutional goals for the senior year.

Institutions need to design first-year assessments to determine what progress is being made toward senior year goals.

Few institutions systematically collect student data at the end of the first college year.

Data should be collected at the end of the first college year to assess the first year and establish a baseline for the sophomore year. A fine example of this recommendation is the National Survey of Student Engagement developed by George Kuh of Indiana University and his colleagues, as discussed elsewhere in this collection.

Most directors of first-year programs have little or no experience in conducting formal assessment.

Partnerships between first-year program directors and institutional researchers/ assessment officers are essential. We have also noted a growing trend on the part of student affairs units to develop their own assessment offices, officers, and initiatives. Given the greater need by our student affairs colleagues to demonstrate that their programs are indeed worth the investment of institutional resources, we believe this development is highly understandable and appropriate. This does not diminish in any way, however, the necessity of partnerships between first-year program directors and institutional researchers.

Each institution has its "assessment-free zones"—areas about which questions are never asked.

"Don't be afraid to ask hard questions—but don't ask questions that you do not have the courage to respond to." This concept of "assessment-free zones" is one discussed by the Policy Center's Co-Director Betsy Barefoot. We have been fascinated not only by the questions our consortia members asked in their assessment process but also by the questions they have NOT asked, and especially by the areas on their campus they chose not to subject to assessment. Unfortunately, the bulk of campus efforts have been to assess relatively low-status elements of the first college year, and not, for example, such high-status elements as the impact of the general education curriculum or the quality of instruction in large first-year courses.

Voluntary assessment may engender stronger support than externally mandated assessment, but it often takes an external mandate to serve as a catalyst for assessment.

We strongly encourage educators to be proactive in determining what matters on their campuses and how best to collect assessment data. Whether assessment is voluntary or involuntary, our findings suggest the only way we can seriously engage faculty in this process is by getting them to raise their key questions rather than our key questions. We emerged from this consortium assessment project believing more strongly than ever in the power of intrinsic motivations to underlie assessment. Our work leads us to be optimistic. Faculty can and will engage in voluntary assessment if they can see some direct connection and payoff between this kind of exercise and increased satisfaction and effectiveness in their most important work as academics.

Where data exist, they are rarely widely distributed, presented in an accessible format, or understood by the campus at large.

Assessment reports should be focused on a few key findings and presented in a user-friendly fashion. In reviewing the work of these consortium institutions, we concluded that not only does the form in which assessment findings are ultimately disseminated matter, but who disseminates these findings is also critical. The more respected and influential the disseminating source, the more likely the information will be considered seriously.

To date, assessment findings have only marginally influenced campus policy decisions.

We encourage educators to take small, gradual steps in the use of assessment data to influence program and policy decisions in the sphere(s) under their control. Unfortunately, we have found that assessment results appear only peripherally in the official language of campuses justifying and explaining their policy development and resource allocations. If we are to move away from this and to build instead a culture of evidence, individuals at every level of the institution—from classroom faculty to unit administrators to the most senior policy makers—have to model this culture. For example, as director of a first-year seminar program, I made sure to communicate with members of the university community about how we were conducting assessment, about what those findings were, and about how we were using those findings to make very specific changes in our first-year course.

Campuses rarely come together in some kind of forum to share what they know about the current state of the first college year and to discuss how it might be improved.

Campuses should consider the sponsorship of a "first-year summit" to share information about first-year programs and outcomes. Let me present two quick examples of such forums, both from North Carolina. Elon College has developed both an assessment and a dissemination process which they call the "Elon Summit." Their first one convened a campus-wide group to discuss the impact of fraternity and sorority subculture on campus life and learning. This meeting was so successful that Elon decided to repeat the exercise and have an "academic summit" to assess the intellectual level of engagement on the campus. These summits are examples of how to create enthusiasm for assessment and related potential for community building. Similarly, in the spring of 2000, North Carolina State University held its first campus-wide gathering to consider the current state of first-year experience practices and initiatives at the University. Again this event at NC State served to increase awareness of the importance and the wide range of discreet activities that enhance the first-year experience. It also contributed to a heightened sense of community for all of the participants.

As I said at the beginning, the "jury is in" for those of us at the Policy Center who have engaged in this pilot assessment process. I hope that after reading this collection, the "jury is in" for you in terms of insights and conclusions you can use to inspire, inform, and direct your own first-year assessment activities. More than anything, we have tried to raise the questions you should be asking. As we all learned in our own liberal arts educations, the questions are often more important than the answers, and the questions underlying the assessment of the first-year experience are the most important starting and ending points of all. We appreciate your joining our two Centers in the asking of these critical questions and your sharing your own unique and important findings.

About the Contributors

Trudy W. Banta   Trudy W. Banta is a national and international authority on assessment, author, researcher, and conference organizer. Since 1983, she has written or edited nine volumes on assessment, contributed 20 chapters to other published works, and written more than 150 articles and reports. She is especially known for her books, *Assessment in Practice* (1996), *Assessment Essentials* (1999), and the bi-monthly periodical *Assessment Update,* which she founded and continues to edit for Jossey-Bass. Banta serves as vice chancellor for planning and institutional improvement and professor of higher education at Indiana University-Purdue University Indianapolis. Prior to assuming her current position, she directed the Center for Assessment Research and Development at the University of Tennessee, Knoxville. Her reputation as an authority on assessment is truly international in scope. She has presented international conferences on the topic of assessing quality in higher education in Australia, Finland, Germany, Hong Kong, the Netherlands, Malaysia, and the United Kingdom, and has given invited addresses at conferences in Canada, China, France, Germany, South Africa, Spain, and the United Arab Emirates.

Betsy O. Barefoot   Betsy O. Barefoot currently serves as co-director of the Policy Center on the First Year of College, located on the campus of Brevard College in Brevard, North Carolina. Prior to assuming this position in October of 1999, Barefoot spent 11 years as co-director for research and publications at the University of South Carolina's National Resource Center for The First-Year Experience, where she conducted ongoing research on the first-year seminar in American higher education and edited a variety of publications on the first-year experience. She is currently a fellow of the Nation Resource Center. Barefoot holds degrees from Duke University (B.A.) and The College of William and Mary (M.Ed. and Ed.D.). In her role with the Policy Center, Barefoot continues her research and publishing on issues related to student retention and the design and delivery of first-year initiatives. She also consults with college campuses around the nation and world on the structure and assessment of first-year programs.

Kinney Baughman holds a master's degree in philosophy from the University of Georgia and a bachelor's degree from Appalachian State University. Baughman was an early adopter of web applications for classroom use and the first instructor at Appalachian to teach a course on web page construction and Internet search strategies. In 1996 he began teaching e-business courses. His area of expertise is using online databases connected by a web interface. Baughman currently serves as director of information technology instruction and research at the Appalachian Regional Development Institute, the service and outreach center at Appalachian State University. He consults with educators and business leaders across western North Carolina.

Kinney Baughman

Trudy Bers is senior director of institutional research, curriculum and strategic planning at Oakton College. She holds advanced degrees from the University of Illinois, Urbana (Ph.D. in political science), Northwestern University (M.M. in marketing and organizational behavior), and Columbia University (M.A. in public law and government). Besides her many contributions to Oakton College, a two-year institution in Des Plaines, Illinois, Bers has made national contributions to higher education through service to the Association for Institutional Research (AIR) and her many scholarly publications. She has served as president of AIR (1995-96), has written the AIR monograph entitled *Effective Reporting,* and has published over 40 articles in professional journals. Bers is an acknowledged expert on the topic of assessment in community colleges.

Trudy Bers

Joseph B. Cuseo is professor of psychology and director of the Freshman Seminar at Marymount College, California. He has authored a monograph and contributed numerous chapters to publications on the first-year experience, and is known for outstanding presentations at national conferences and contributions to the national listserv on the first-year experience. He is a 10-time recipient of the Faculty Member of the Year Award on his home campus, and has received the Outstanding First-Year Student Advocate Award from the National Resource Center for The First-Year Experience and Students in Transition.

Joseph B. Cuseo

Glenn Detrick has been involved in management education for the past 22 years and has been co-chairman of EBI since its inception in 1994. He served as associate dean for administration and director of the MBA program at the John M. Olin School of Business (Washington University) from 1976 to 1990 and, prior to that, as Assistant Dean for the Undergraduate Program. Detrick left the Olin School in 1990

Glenn Detrick

to become vice president for educational programs at the Graduate Management Admissions Council (GMAC). There, he was involved in the establishment of international student recruiting forums in Europe and Asia and for the development and delivery of a number of seminars for business school administrators on topics such as managing change, TQM, and assessment. Since leaving GMAC in 1993, Detrick has consulted widely on MBA curriculum development, strategic planning, faculty development, and other issues related to management education.

Nancy J. Evans   Nancy J. Evans is a professor in the Department of Educational Leadership and Policy Studies and coordinator of the higher education program at Iowa State University. She received her Ph.D. in 1978 from the University of Missouri-Columbia. Evans has edited, co-edited, and co-authored several books, including *Student Development in College: Theory, Research, and Practice, The State of the Art of Professional Preparation and Practice in Student Affairs: Another Look,* and *Toward Acceptance: Sexual Orientation Issues on Campus.* She also has numerous journal articles and book chapters to her credit and has presented over 100 programs and papers at professional association meetings. In recognition of her scholarly work, Evans was awarded the Contribution to Knowledge Award and was named a Senior Scholar in 1998 by the American College Personnel Association. She is president of the American College Personnel Association (2001-02).

Peter Ewell   Peter Ewell is a Senior Associate at the National Center for Higher Education Management Systems (NCHEMS), a research and development center founded to improve the management effectiveness of colleges and universities. A member of the staff since 1981, Ewell's work focuses on assessing institutional effectiveness and the outcomes of college and involves both research and direct consulting with institutions and state systems on collecting and using assessment information in planning, evaluation, and budgeting. He is a principal partner in the Pew Forum on Undergraduate Learning. He has consulted with more than 375 colleges and universities and 22 state systems of higher education on topics including assessment, program review, enrollment management, and student retention. In addition, Ewell has authored six books and numerous articles on the topic of improving undergraduate instruction through the assessment of student outcomes. Among his publications are commissioned papers for many agencies, and he has spoken widely on this topic at both national and international conferences. A graduate of Haverford College, he received his Ph.D. in Political Science from Yale University in 1976 and served on the faculty of the University of Chicago.

John N. Gardner is senior fellow of the National Resource **John N. Gardner**
Center for The First-Year Experience and Students in Transition, which he founded in 1986, and distinguished professor
emeritus of library and information science at the University
of South Carolina. Previously, he served as executive director
of both the first-year seminar course University 101 from 1974–
1999, and the National Resource Center from 1986–99. In his
capacity as senior fellow with the National Resource Center,
Gardner is actively involved in hosting and presenting at Center conferences, seminars, workshops, and teleconferences. He
also remains very involved in the Center's scholarship and
research activities such as its monograph series and other publishing activities. Since October 1999, Gardner has served as
executive director of the Policy Center on the First Year of
College, based at Brevard College, Brevard, North Carolina.
He is also appointed there as Distinguished Professor of Educational Leadership.

George D. Kuh is a leading authority on assessment in **George D. Kuh**
higher education. He is Chancellor's Professor of Higher
Education at Indiana University Bloomington, past president
of the Association for the Study of Higher Education (ASHE),
an author, and director of several national projects focused
on assessment issues. He directs the College Student Experiences Questionnaire Program and the National Survey of
Student Engagement, an annual survey of college first-year
and senior students co-sponsored by The Pew Charitable
Trusts, the Carnegie Foundation for the Advancement of
Teaching, and The Pew Forum on Undergraduate Learning.
Kuh has published some 200 books, chapters, and articles.
He has made hundreds of presentations on topics related to
college and university cultures, student engagement, assessment, and institutional improvement. Kuh has been honored with numerous awards for his work in higher education. He recently received an award for research achievement from ASHE. Previously the American College Personnel Association recognized him for his contribution to knowledge and named him a Senior Scholar and Senior Scholar
Diplomate. The National Association of Student Personnel
Administrators cited his contributions to literature and research and honored him for outstanding contribution to student affairs through teaching. In 1998, he was identified as
one of the Ten Most Influential People in Student Affairs.

Jodi H. Levine is assistant vice provost for university **Jodi H. Levine**
studies, Temple University. Levine has coupled extensive
campus-based experience as a practitioner and undergraduate educator at Temple University since 1990 with comparable extensive experience as a researcher, writer, speaker,

and advocate for educational improvement, most notably through the initiation and refinement of learning communities. She is editor of *Learning Communities: New Structures, New Partnerships for Learning* (1999), published by the National Resource Center for The First-Year Experience and Students in Transition at the University of South Carolina, and co-author of *Learning Communities: A Practical Guide to Winning Support, Organizing for Change, and Implementing Programs* (1999), published by Jossey-Bass. As a researcher, she also has experience in qualitative studies conducting assessments, for example, of Temple University's "studies in race" core curriculum in addition to her separate studies of learning communities and first-year seminar initiatives. Besides directing learning communities, she has responsibility for coordinating Supplemental Instruction and first-year seminar programs at Temple.

Brenda C. Moore   Brenda C. Moore is director of freshman and senior programs at Gardner-Webb University in Boiling Springs, North Carolina. Since 1996, Brenda has tirelessly worked to build effective support programs for first-year students at Gardner-Webb University. She holds a graduate degree from East Carolina University. After a "first career" as a public school teacher and reading specialist, she now combines program administration and classroom teaching at the college level.

Catherine A. Palomba   Catherine A. Palomba is director emeritus of institutional research and academic assessment at Ball State University (BSU). Previously, she was a research analyst at the Center for Naval Analyses in Alexandria, Virginia and an associate professor of economics at West Virginia University (WVU). While at WVU, she published several refereed articles and received two awards as an outstanding teacher. In 1998, the American Productivity and Quality Center recognized BSU's assessment program as a "best practice" institution for assessing learning outcomes. Catherine has co-authored *Assessment Essentials: Planning, Implementing, and Improving Assessment in Higher Education*, published by Jossey-Bass (1999) and *Assessing Student Competence in Accredited Disciplines: Pioneering Approaches to Assessment in Higher Education* (2001), published by Stylus Publishing, LLC. Palomba earned a bachelor's degree from the Baruch School of the City College of New York (1965), a master's degree from the University of Minnesota (1966), and a Ph.D. from Iowa State University (1969), all in economics.

Joseph A. Pica   Joseph A. Pica is co-founder and Co-Chairman of Educational Benchmarking, Inc. (EBI). He received his Ed.D. in higher education administration from Indiana University.

Pica spent 8 years as a residence life professional, and 14 years in graduate management education. He served as assistant dean and director of the MBA Program at Indiana University from 1986 to 1997 and as a member of the Board of Directors for the Graduate Management Admission Council (GMAC) and on the Board of Trustees for the Consortium for Graduate Study in Management. He is currently a guest lecturer for the Indiana University Kelley School of Business.

Stephen Porter

Stephen Porter is currently the director of institutional research at Wesleyan University. Before accepting that position he worked in institutional research and evaluation at the School of Nursing, University of Maryland, Baltimore, and the University of Maryland, College Park. He holds an M.A. and Ph.D. in Political Science from the University of Rochester and a B.A. from Rice University. He is a frequent and highly respected presenter at institutional research conferences and has published in several educational research journals.

Karl Schilling

Karl Schilling currently serves as the deputy director for policy at the State Council of Higher Education for Virginia where he is involved in analyzing data and formulating higher education policy recommendations for the Virginia Governor and General Assembly. He provides leadership to the policy area on issues such as student graduation and retention rates, funding, general education requirements, and assessments of academic programs and student outcomes. He is former director of the American Association for Higher Education (AAHE)'s Assessment Forum, where his leadership helped establish this event as the premier conference on higher education assessment. Prior to his appointments at AAHE and SHEV, Schilling served as Associate Dean and Associate Professor of Interdisciplinary Studies at the Western College of Miami University (Ohio). Schilling has authored eight funded grants, several of which are focused on the assessment of liberal education programs, and authored 18 articles published in professional journals, most of which focus on assessing the student experience—particularly in relation to students' intellectual and personal development. He has consulted with over 50 higher education institutions on development of powerful liberal education programs and assessment of student learning outcomes.

Charles Schroeder

Charles Schroeder is a professor of higher education and formerly the chief student affairs officer of the University of Missouri at Columbia. Because he has been recognized as a prophet in his own land, he has been called upon for the highest leadership roles at the national level, serving, for example, for two terms as the president of the American College Personnel Association. He is also president of the ACPA Educational Leadership Foundation. He is widely published in such areas as scholarship of residence halls, student personality types and learning styles, learning communities assessment, applying Continuous Quality Improvement (CQI), and best practices in student affairs administration and leadership. He convened a group in 1994 which produced the landmark Student Learning Imperative, a philosophical blueprint for an enormously important shift in the focus of student affairs professionals in the 1990s that is aligned with the primary academic missions of the institutions in which they serve.

John H. Schuh   John H. Schuh is professor of educational leadership and department chair at Iowa State University. He is the author, co-author, or editor of over 150 publications. His newest publication, an edited book, *Educational Programming and Student Learning in College and University Residence Halls,* was released by Association of College and University Housing Officers–International (ACUHO-I) in December 1999. He has served as editor and chair of the American College Personnel Association (ACPA) Media Board and has served as a member of the editorial board of the *Journal of College Student Development.* Currently he is editor in chief of the *New Directions for Student Services Sourcebook* series and is associate editor of the *Journal of College Student Development.* He has served on other editorial boards including the editorial board of *Net Results* (the National Association of Student Personnel Administrator's electronic journal) and *The Journal of College Student Recruitment and Retention.* Schuh has made over 155 presentations and speeches to campus-based, regional and national meetings. He has served as a consultant to 30 colleges, universities, and other organizations and on the governing boards of ACPA, NASPA (twice), and ACUHO-I (twice). Recently he was selected to join the Evaluator Corps of the North Central Association of Colleges and Schools. Schuh has received the Contribution to Knowledge Award and the Presidential Service Award from ACPA, the Contribution to Research or Literature award from NASPA, and the Leadership and Service and S. Earl Thompson Awards from ACUHO-I. He has been elected as a Senior Scholar Diplomate by ACPA and was also chosen as one of ACPA's 75 Diamond Honorees in 1999.

Linda Suskie   Linda Suskie is coordinator of assessment at Towson University and a past director of the American Association for Higher Education's Assessment Forum. Her work as an author, practitioner, teacher, and scholar has added depth and specificity to the national movement in higher education assessment. After serving as the Forum director in 1999-2000, Linda returned to Millersville University of Pennsylvania to serve as director of planning, assessment, and analysis. She concurrently serves as a CHE Fellow for the Middle States Commission on Higher Education. Her 25 years of higher education experience include work in assessment, accreditation, strategic planning, and continuous improvement. She has taught graduate courses and facilitated workshops and retreats on these subjects. Linda is the author of *Questionnaire Survey Research: What Works,* published by the Association for Institutional Research, and has presented on survey research, equity in assessment, and other assessment principles and tools. She holds an M.A. in Educational Measurement and Statistics from the University of Iowa and a B.A. in Quantitative Studies from Johns Hopkins University.

Randy L. Swing

Randy L. Swing serves as co-director of the Policy Center on the First Year of College, located at Brevard College in Brevard, North Carolina. In his work at the Policy Center, Swing coordinates five higher education regional consortia in Georgia, North Carolina, and Virginia focusing on assessment of first-year programs. He is directly involved in the development of assessment instruments and in the Center's national dissemination of information about assessment methodologies. Until 1999, he worked for 20 years in various first-year programs at Appalachian State University including the Freshman Seminar Program; Early Start Summer Program; Academic Advising Center for first-year students and sophomores; Summer Preview Program for marginally prepared students; and Upward Bound program serving low-income, first-generation students from rural Appalachia. Most recently, as founding director of the assessment office, he developed and initiated a longitudinal, campus-wide assessment program with focus on learning outcomes. Prior to earning a doctoral degree in higher education from the University of Georgia, he earned his M.A. and Ed.S. degrees in student development from Appalachian State University and a B.A. in psychology from the University of North Carolina – Charlotte. He serves on the Review Board for the *Journal on Excellence in College Teaching* and frequently serves as a grant reader for the U.S. Department of Education. In 1999 he received a National Science Foundation Summer Fellowship to study public opinion of educational policy. He is a fellow of the National Resource Center for The First-Year Experience and Students in Transition.

Patrick T. Terenzini

Patrick T. Terenzini is professor and senior scientist, Center for the Study of Higher Education at Pennsylvania State University. His career in higher education spans more

than 25 years as an administrator and faculty member—
including nine years as director of institutional research and,
later, assistant to the president for planning at the State University of New York at Albany. He has held teaching positions at Dean Junior College, Syracuse University, and the
University of Georgia before joining Penn State's Center for
the Study of Higher Education in 1990. Terenzini has published more than 100 articles in refereed journals and made
numerous presentations at national scholarly and professional conferences. He is co-author (with Ernest T. Pascarella) of *How College Affects Students,* an award-winning
review of the research on the effects of college on students.
His other contributions to the literature of higher education include serving as editor-in-chief of *New Directions for
Institutional Research,* Consulting Editor of *Research in Higher
Education,* and Associate Editor of *Higher Education: Handbook of Theory and Research.* In tribute to Terenzini's leadership and contribution to research, he was named a Senior
Scholar Diplomate of the American College Personnel Association and presented the Outstanding Service Award by
the Association for Institutional Research. Additionally, he
has served as president of the Association for the Study of
Higher Education.

M. Lee Upcraft   M. Lee Upcraft is one of the "long marchers" in this
national movement to call more attention to first-year students, and his work as co-author of *The Freshman Year Experience,* Jossey-Bass, 1989, has been particularly influential
in providing an intellectual context for this reform effort.
Upcraft took early retirement from his position as Assistant Vice President for Student Affairs at The Pennsylvania
State University six years ago so that he could concentrate
on his scholarship, particularly in the field of assessment.
He is currently a research associate in the Center for the
Study of Higher Education at Penn State and remains active as a supervisor of doctoral students and faculty member as affiliate professor emeritus. He has more than 35 years
of experience as an academic and student affairs administrator, assessment practitioner and scholar, and faculty
member. His many other scholarly published writings are
on the topics of residence halls, student retention, assessment in student affairs, student demographics, and the first-
year experience.

Titles of Interest to Assessment Professionals from the National Resource Center for The First-Year Experience & Students in Transition

Monograph 33. *Proving and Improving: Strategies for Assessing the First College Year*. Randy L. Swing, Editor. Drawn from the First-Year Assessment Listserv, which is hosted by the Policy Center on the First Year of College and the National Resource Center, this collection provides essays by the nation's best theorists and practitioners of first-year college assessment. Contributors outline the essentials of effective assessment efforts, provide a philosophical rationale for those essentials, describe methods and strategies for assessment, and provide examples designed for institutions and specific programs. Written from the perspective of practitioners in a wide range of disciplines and organizational structures, these essays are accessible and valuable to the novice and veteran practitioner alike. 140 pages. ISBN 1-889271-37-3. $20.00.

Monograph 25. *Exploring the Evidence: Reporting Outcomes of First-Year Seminars, Volume II*. Betsy O. Barefoot, Editor-in-Chief. Produced with the financial support of the Houghton Mifflin Company, Volume II of *Exploring the Evidence* reviews research conducted on 50 first-year seminars. This collection is a valuable resource for seminar directors and others who are seeking models for research design and evidence of the effectiveness of this familiar course genre. Research outcomes described in this volume include improved rates of retention and graduation, higher student grade point averages, increased levels of student satisfaction, and positive changes in faculty attitudes and their repertoire of teaching strategies. 120 pages. ISBN 1-899271-25-X. $30.00.

The Journal of The First-Year Experience and Students in Transition. The only journal dedicated to the collegiate success and survival of students in transition, the *Journal of The First-Year Experience and Students in Transition* publishes definitive scholarship by respected higher education researchers about the factors that relate to student success and survival. If you are interested or involved in your institution's programming for first-year, transfer, or senior students, you will want to know how the latest research can inform practice to enhance student success. ISSN 1053-203X. $40.00.

Guidelines for Evaluating The First-Year Experience at Two-Year Colleges and *Guidelines for Evaluating The First-Year Experience at Four-Year Colleges*. 2nd Edition. John N. Gardner, Betsy O. Barefoot, and Randy L. Swing. These guidelines provide institutions with a framework for assessing the first-year experience on their own campuses. Originally developed by John Gardner in 1990, *Guidelines for Evaluating The First-Year Experience* has been revised and updated by the staff of the Policy Center on the First Year of College with input from 65 institutions participating in five regional consortia focused on first-year assessment issues. *Guidelines* is now available in two special editions, one focusing on two-year institutions and one focusing on four-year institutions. If you are looking for a way to evaluate the first-year experience on your campus, make *Guidelines* your starting point! 24 pages. $7.00 each/$5.00 each when sold in units of 10.

Use the order form on the next page to order any of these titles from the National Resource Center.

Use this form to order additional copies of this monograph or to order other titles from the National Resource Center for The First-Year Experience & Students in Transition.

Prices advertised in this publication are subject to change.

Item	Quantity	Price	Total
Monograph 33. *Proving and Improving*		$20.00	
Monograph 25. *Exploring the Evidence, Vol. II*		$30.00	
Monograph 11. *Exploring the Evidence, Vol. I*		$20.00	
Guidelines for Evaluating The First-Year Experience at Two-Year Colleges		$7.00 each $5.00 each/10*	
Guidelines for Evaluating The First-Year Experience at Four-Year Colleges		$7.00 each $5.00 each/10*	
Journal of The First-Year Experience & Students in Transition		$40.00/year	
*Call for shipping charges on this item.	Shipping & Handling		
	Total		

Shipping Charges:	Order Amount	Shipping Cost
U.S. & Canada	$0 - $50	$ 5.50 US
	$50 - $150	$ 8.00 US
	over $150	$10.00 US
Foreign	*for any amount*	$20.00 US

Name _____   Department _____

Institution _____   Telephone _____

Address _____

City _____ State/Province _____ Postal Code _____

E-mail Address _____

Select your option payable to the University of South Carolina:

❏ Check Enclosed   ❏ Institutional Purchase Order   Purchase Order No. _____

Credit Card: ❏ VISA   ❏ MasterCard   ❏ DISCOVER

Card No. _____

Name of Cardholder _____

Signature _____

Mail this form to: National Resource Center for The First-Year Experience & Students in Transition, University of South Carolina, 1728 College Street, Columbia, SC 29208. Phone (803) 777-6029. FAX (803) 777-4699. E-mail burtonp@gwm.sc.edu Federal ID 57-6001153.